This is Michael Ots at his best! Mak how we make meaning out of life - purpose, and love, to our longing world. He shows us why the Christian faith .... of life – in a way that is accessible, easy to read and thought provoking. Read it for yourselves and then give it to everyone you know who is trying to make sense out of life!

Rebecca Manley Pippert, author, *Stay Salt* and *Out of the Salt Shaker*

Honest, refreshing, engaging, and powerful – if you're genuinely interested in making sense of life's deepest questions, this book is a great place to start.

Andy Bannister, Director, the Solas Centre; author and speaker

In his latest book, Making Sense of Life, *Michael Ots weaves together a compelling case for the Christian faith, pointing us in the right direction to find true purpose and meaning. I highly recommend reading this book and sharing it with others.*

Dr Amy Orr-Ewing, author and speaker

Michael Ots has spent 20 years speaking and listening on university campuses across Britain and Europe. He knows what the big questions of life are, and if you turn to the contents page I'm certain you'll find at least three chapter headings

which deal with subjects that you find both beckoning and bewildering. The chapters themselves are full of wisdom, illustration and breadth, which did not disappoint. I thoroughly recommend this most timely book, as we all try and make sense of a post-COVID world.

Rico Tice, Minister, All Souls Church; co-founder, Christianity Explored

Many years ago I saw a poster as I entered Heathrow airport near London, which had an image of a plane at take-off and the text underneath, "Where in the world are you going?" Michael Ots is answering the same question in this book. He provides honest, thoughtful and deeply satisfying answers to the most urgent deeply-felt existential questions of our day... answers which are found in the person of Jesus Christ and all that He has to offer to those trying to make sense of the world and our place in it. The honest seeker will find great riches here. Enjoy!

Lindsay Brown, Director, Fellowship of Evangelists in the Universities of Europe

Michael Ots is an astute observer of society who has carefully analysed the aspirations of contemporary people and made a compelling case for considering the Christian approach to life.

Ajith Fernando, Teaching Director, Youth for Christ, Sri Lanka; author, *Discipling in a Multicultural World*

Making
Sense
of Life

MICHAEL OTS

Copyright © 2021 by Michael Ots

First published in Great Britain in 2021

British Library Cataloguing in Publication Data
A record for this book is available from the British Library

ISBN: 978-1-913896-55-3

Cover designed by Chevonne Elbourne

Typeset by Pete Barnsley (CreativeHoot)

Printed in Denmark by Nørhaven

10Publishing, a division of 10ofthose.com
Unit C, Tomlinson Road, Leyland, PR25 2DY, England

Email: info@10ofthose.com
Website: www.10ofthose.com

1 3 5 7 10 8 6 4 2

Contents

Acknowledgements

I used to quip that my books seem to come out like the Olympics – every four years. That cycle seemed to have been broken though, as it is now five years since the publication of my last book, *But Is It True?* However, with the delay of the Tokyo Olympics, I seem to have inadvertently kept to this pattern!

I was once asked why I didn't write more often – one reason is that all my books started life as talks that were given at universities over a period of several years. I am therefore thankful to the many university student groups around Europe that have invited me to speak on these topics, in particular to the Christian Union in the University of Leeds who first came up with many of the talk titles that now form the chapters of this book. I'm also grateful to the many students who have asked insightful and challenging questions after my talks. In doing so they have encouraged to me go back and think even more deeply about each issue. As it is not possible to hold a Q&A after each chapter of the book, I have sought to anticipate and incorporate many of these questions as we go along.

Another reason for not writing more often is that I need to give my friends a break! Writing a book like this really is a team effort, and I am deeply grateful to all those who have contributed to the process.

Many friends have generously given their time to read through the manuscript and provide helpful feedback. I'm so thankful to Dick and Rose Dowsett, Rod Statham, Tim Dixon, Bruce Gillingham, Amy Orr-Ewing, Andy Bannister, Peter Dray, and Niv Lobo. Our neighbours at Millbank in Marlow gave us many opportunities for stimulating conversations (normally over drinks at 'The Docks') about a number of these issues. In particular, thank you to Mark Stafford and Chris Funnell for reading through the book and giving your feedback (and for lending us your boat!)

I'm thankful to those who provided some wonderful locations in which to write: Doreen and Roger for the use of their incredible cottage and Tim and Joyce for their amazing summer house. Rodda's clotted cream and pasties from Bray's and K's in Redruth provided much of the energy needed for the job in hand!

Thank you so much to Mary Navey for reading through the manuscript several times and turning my scrawl into something more appropriate for publication! I sometimes wonder if, like films, books should have 'outtakes'? If so, Mary could provide some hilarious examples.

Thank you to my editor, Julie Hatherall, for your diligent work and your patience, and to 10ofthose for your incredible work publishing and distributing so many helpful books.

Finally and most importantly, thank you to Rebecca: for putting up with me being so often distracted by this book and for your continual love and support on the journey.

Making sense of life

It was 2 a.m. and I found myself in tears as I sat on a mattress on the floor of my friend's office in New Zealand. I had intended to go to sleep hours beforehand, but I had made the mistake of starting to read Paul Kalanithi's memoir, *When Breath Becomes Air*. It is one of the most profound, moving and heartbreaking books I have ever read.

In the book, he vividly describes his own battle with cancer alongside his work as a neurosurgeon, his marriage and the birth of their child. Despite the fact that I read the entire book knowing that he was going to die (for it had been published posthumously), I found myself willing there to be a different ending. As his wife took over to write the last chapter, describing their final hours together, I found I couldn't hold back the tears.

As he faced up to the reality of his own mortality, Paul Kalanithi started to revaluate his own beliefs about the world. Being a young medical student, he had embraced a materialistic view of the world, as he explained: 'I, like most scientific types, came to believe in the possibility of the material conception of reality, an ultimately scientific worldview that would grant a complete metaphysics, minus outmoded concepts like souls, God, and bearded white men in robes.'[1] That is, he believed that the only things that really existed were those that could be explained scientifically. Matter was all that existed; there was nothing more, certainly no God or spiritual realm.

While I often find such a view can be very popular in a lecture hall, it is harder to sustain it in the day-to-day realities of life. All of us will go through moments when we are forced to face up to life's big questions.

There can be any number of triggers for these moments of existential wondering.

For some, it is the reality of death. Living through a global pandemic certainly has a way of making us ask questions.

For others, it is the wonder of life that gets them thinking. One of the deepest conversations that I ever had with one of my neighbours was the day his first child was born. Being confronted with the miraculous bundle of life he now held in his arms had made him ask questions about his own life and the purpose of it.

Beauty is another common trigger. One of my favourite places in the world is the Lauterbrunnen Valley in Switzerland. It was here that J.R.R. Tolkien found inspiration for the magical, elvish land of Rivendell in *The Lord of the Rings*. It's not hard to see why. A total of seventy-two waterfalls cascade down the 400-metre-high cliffs on either side of the lush green valley, while the snowclad 4000-metre-high summit of the Jungfrau towers above.

I remember sitting at the edge of one of those cliffs one summer's evening to watch the sunset. As I was drinking in the view, I got chatting to a couple who had just appeared nearby. Although we had never met before, the beauty of the scene in front of us was such that we ended up having the kind of deep conversation that, for the average Brit, would normally take years of friendship (or a lot of alcohol) to achieve! Was this beauty that we were appreciating just the end result of time and chance? Or did it point to something beyond itself?

While such beauty may be a trigger for some, the utter brokenness of the world causes others to question what life is all about. For many in the West, the real shock of the Covid-19 pandemic was that, for the first time, we couldn't just switch off the TV news and go back to normal life. There was no 'normal life'. Many have suffered immense loss, battled illness or suffered from the terrible impact of isolation and loneliness. Most of us westerners had homes to live in, food to eat and Netflix to watch (which was a lot more than many in the world had), but something seemed to be missing. There has to be more to life than simply not dying, but what is it?

Concern about the injustices and inequalities of our world can cause us to think more deeply about life too. Why is our world so unfair and how can we improve it? Many of us want to feel that we are part of something bigger than ourselves.

Changes in life's circumstances, like redundancy or retirement, also lead us to ask big questions. In our society, so much of our identity is bound up with our job. 'What do you do?' is usually the first question we ask someone when we meet for the first time. While there is nothing necessarily wrong with this, a problem arises when we don't have anything 'to do'. Who are we then? My wife was recently chatting to a colleague who, like her, was facing the very real threat of redundancy in the aviation industry – a job that they both love. Just a couple of weeks before, he had seemed so secure and confident. Now he was crippled with anxiety and living with the help of antidepressants.

How do we make sense of life in times like this? Why do we think that life is so valuable? Where do we find a true and lasting sense of identity? Why do we long for meaningful and lasting relationships? From where does our concern about this physical world come? Why do we feel that life is so broken? Why is it so hard to live without hope? How can we experience real freedom?

In addition, where can we turn to in order to find answers to these questions? Does our view of the world account for these things that we care so much about?

As I chat to university students across Europe, I have found that many have a similar worldview to the one that Paul Kalanithi had. Most wouldn't think much about God – if at all. It's not that they are hostile to God, like a previous generation of angry New Atheists would have been. They simply don't see how God has much to do with anything.

Ultimately, if they were pushed, they would likely say that the only stuff that really exists is what we can see, touch and test. If we want to discover truth about our world, they would state that it is the objectivity of science, rather than religion, that will give us the answers.

The technical term for such an idea is *materialism* – the belief that matter is ultimately all that exists. Most wouldn't use the term, and some maybe haven't even heard of it. Yet, for many, it describes the functional view they have of the world.

Most people find that holding this view of the world works just fine for the majority of their life. It is easy at university to be a materialist, as many in academia hold to the same view. We find that we can get through our studies just fine, without any appeal to the supernatural to understand our course. It is easy to keep holding the view after we graduate as well. After all, if you live in a Western country, materialism is the shared assumption of many in society. We can get a job, buy a house, get married, have kids and lead a successful life without ever having to think about God.

However, when life's circumstances cause us to start asking some of the bigger questions, does our view of the world give us answers? Does it account for the things that *really* matter?

Paul Kalanithi ultimately found that it doesn't. He discovered that his functional atheism just didn't explain those things that he really cared about. He concluded, 'The problem, however, eventually became evident; to make science the arbiter of metaphysics is to banish not only God from the world but also love, hate, meaning

– to consider a world that is self-evidently not the world we live in.'[2]

So much of what is most important to us in life is very hard to explain by science alone. Over the coming chapters, we will look at some of these things: our desire for happiness, love, freedom and hope; our need for identity and purpose; our concerns about human rights; our society and the environment. We will see how materialism struggles to provide answers for *why* these things are so important.

One of the longest running and most successful advertising slogans in history is: 'There are some things money can't buy … for everything else there's Mastercard.' Fascinatingly, it is based on reminding viewers of the limitations of the very thing they are seeking to advertise! We may want to say something similar about science. Just as there are some things that money can't buy, there are some things that science can't explain. This is not to belittle science or scientists. It is simply to realise that there might be more to life than meets the eye.

Could it be that all these things are more fully explained by taking into account the possibility of a God? And not just any God, but the God who revealed himself as Jesus? This possibility may seem a surprising direction to take. While love, freedom, human rights and the environment figure very highly in our concerns, God is often a long way down the list (if he is there at all). Yet I hope to demonstrate that it is the Christian faith that makes best sense of what matters most.

A note about the rest of the book

While you can read this book in the typical manner – from cover to cover – you may also read it in whatever order you like. Feel free to start with whichever chapter interests you the most.

As you read, you'll notice that, at some point in each chapter, I quote from the Bible. I do so quite unapologetically. If you want to understand Christianity, you really need to look at Jesus Christ. (The clue is in the name – *Christ*-ianity!) To understand Jesus, the best place to start is one of the contemporary accounts of his life, which are often referred to as 'the gospels'. They form the first four books (Matthew, Mark, Luke and John) of the second half of the Bible (which we call the New Testament). We will look particularly at these books.

If you have questions about their historical accuracy, then you may want to look at my book *But Is It True?*[3] Yet don't feel you need to deal with all of these questions before you can go any further. Let me explain why.

I recently bought a new pair of binoculars because our apartment overlooked the River Thames and I wanted to be able to watch the wildlife on and around it. The salesman spent a long time telling me all the technical specifications of these particular binoculars and why they were better than the others – and worth spending considerably more money on too! Not knowing much about binoculars, his words made little sense to me. What really sold them to me was that when I picked them up and had a look through them, I could instantly see that they were indeed superior to all the rest.

In the same way, if you want to know whether the Bible is worth taking seriously, there are two ways you can do this: you can ask technical questions about its accuracy and historicity, or you can start by looking into it and see what you find. As I have done both, I have not only found that the Bible stands up to historical scrutiny, but also discovered that it tells a story that – compared to all others – really does make best sense of the things that matter most.

1

Making sense of humanity

What makes humans worthy of human rights?

The 2010 film *Made in Dagenham* retells the true story of one group of women in 1960s England and their fight for equal pay. Working as machinists in the Ford car plant in Dagenham, they are angered by the fact that they are being paid less than their male colleagues for equally skilled work, and they decide to strike. Despite having to overcome many barriers, their cause gains momentum until it is noticed by the government, finally leading to the Equal Pay Act of 1970.

It is just one of numerous films that dramatise the battles that have been fought in the area of human rights. *Amazing Grace* deals with the abolition of the slave trade, *Invictus* with the ending of apartheid and *Selma* with the civil rights movement, to name just three.

There have been many victories for human rights in the last two hundred years. Each is worth celebrating, and their stories need telling, for all of them have come at a cost. William Wilberforce lost his health; Nelson Mandela, his freedom; and Martin Luther King, his life.

However, that doesn't mean that there are no more battles to fight. Slavery still exists. Discrimination still occurs. Racism certainly hasn't been eradicated. The fight for human rights goes on.

We'll think more about some of these ongoing battles in chapter four. In order to do that, we need to ask some more fundamental questions here: why do we so easily assume that we *have* human rights? Where does that assumption come from? Are we even worthy of the rights we claim to have? Why should humans be treated with such dignity when they themselves often haven't treated each other or the world in that way?

How much are we worth?

Behind our battle for human rights is the belief that human life is valuable. Yet how much are we actually worth? Apparently, about £5!

Even if we have not assumed ourselves to be worth millions like a Premier League footballer, it still comes as a bit of a shock to realise that, from a material point of view, we are worth little more than a pint of beer! However, if you were to break down the average human body into its constituent elements and sell them to a chemist, then that's all you'd get. In the average human body, there is, apparently, enough iron to make a fifteen-centimetre nail; enough sulphur to cure a dog of fleas; enough carbon to make 900 pencils; enough potassium to fire a toy cannon; enough fat to make seven bars of soap (possibly more in mine!); enough phosphorous to tip the end of 2200 matches; and enough water to fill a ten-gallon tank.

We may laugh at such an idea – we know that there is more to us than that. But if the only thing that really exists is physical matter, then how can we be anything more than that? If matter is all there is, then why do we matter?

Francis Crick is remembered for being one of the two scientists who discovered the structure of DNA. He was also a materialist, as is evident from his writing: '"You," your joys and your sorrows, your memories and your ambitions, your sense of personal identity and free will, are in fact no more than the behaviour of a vast assembly of nerve cells and their associated molecules ... "You're nothing but a pack of neurons."'[4] I do sometimes wonder, though, what response any of us would get if we declared to our loved ones on Valentine's Day, 'To my darling pack of neurons, my nerve cells love you very much!'?

Crick was not alone in dismissing the idea of intrinsic human value. Stephen Pinker, the Canadian cognitive psychologist, wrote in *The New Republic* of the 'stupidity of dignity'.[5] Yuval Noah Harari, the Israeli historian and atheist, says in his book *Sapiens*, 'Homo sapiens has no natural rights, just as spiders, hyenas and chimpanzees have no natural rights.'[6] Peter Singer, the Australian moral philosopher, takes the view to some uncomfortable conclusions. He advocates not only for abortion, but also for infanticide. He suggests that killing infants 'cannot be equated with killing normal human beings, or any other self-conscious beings. No infant – disabled or not – has as strong a claim to life as beings capable of seeing themselves as distinct entities existing over time.'[7] He proposes that until twenty-eight days after birth an infant could be killed because it is still a non-person.

While I respect Crick, Pinker and Singer for their honesty about what they truly think, it also causes me to ask questions. Can anyone really live as if such things were actually true? If not, why is that? Most of us find this materialistic approach to reality totally unliveable.

Where do human rights come from?

In his superb book *Dominion*,[8] Tom Holland (the historian – not Spiderman) shows that human rights didn't just appear by chance. They were a direct consequence of Christianity and its influence upon history that has come to us via the Enlightenment.[9] In contrast, he says no other belief system even comes close to giving us any justification for these rights.

To discover how exactly Christianity gave us the idea of human rights, let's look at an encounter in the Bible between Jesus and a man with an obvious physical disability. This tells us both where human rights come from and why they are important.

The incident takes place in Jesus' home town. So many have come to hear Jesus speak that the crowd spills out of the house and on to the street. Among the crowd that day are four friends who bring with them a disabled friend on a stretcher. Unperturbed by the crowd, they come up with an ingenious way of getting their friend to Jesus. They go up onto the flat roof of the building and dig through the ceiling before lowering their friend into the room. We read:

> *When Jesus saw their faith, he said to the paralysed man, 'Son, your sins are forgiven.'*
>
> *Now some teachers of the law were sitting there, thinking to themselves, 'Why does this fellow talk like that? He's blaspheming! Who can forgive sins but God alone?'*
>
> *Immediately Jesus knew in his spirit that this was what they were thinking in their hearts, and he said to them, 'Why are you thinking these things? Which is easier: to say to this paralysed man, "Your sins are forgiven," or to say, "Get up, take your mat and walk"? But I want you to know that the Son of Man has authority on earth to forgive sins.' So he said to the man, 'I tell you, get up, take your mat and go home.' He got up, took his mat and walked out in full view of them all. This amazed everyone and they praised God, saying, 'We have never seen anything like this!'[10]*

This incident in Jesus' life, while perhaps amusing to picture, should also strike us as a rather surprising one. Why do the people have to resort to digging through the roof to get their friend to Jesus? In our Western society, we make extra effort to try to ensure that people are not unduly disadvantaged by any disability (though I am frequently made aware that we could often do much better ...). Normally, we would make provision for a person with obvious physical disabilities with, for example, an assigned parking space, wheelchair access and an allocated place for them to sit. Such people don't have to resort to criminal damage to gain access to a popular public venue!

Yet that has not always been the case. In the culture of Jesus' day, those with disabilities would have been noticeably marginalised in their society. As well as facing physical disadvantages, they would have also had to endure the rejection of others. Disability was a source of shame for it was assumed that the person's disability was somehow deserved, due to something they or their parents had done. Such a view still exists in some parts of the world today. When I visited an orphanage for children with severe disabilities in an East Asian country, I was shocked to hear that none of their parents had died. Instead, the children had all been abandoned. When I asked one of the staff why this was the case, they explained that the concept of karma can lead to the idea that misfortune in life is somehow deserved.

So why are people with disabilities now afforded rights that they were once denied? Why do we care about those who would have, at one time, been marginalised and disadvantaged? The answer is that we live in a world that is still reverberating with the shock waves of Jesus' story. Though we often don't realise it, our world today has been massively affected by the Christian revolution.

You may expect me, as a Christian, to say that. However, interestingly, this is also commonly accepted by many thinkers who are not Christians. In his book *Sapiens*, Yuval Noah Harari admits that the very concept of human rights is based on the Christian faith. He says, 'The Americans got the idea of equality from Christianity which argues that every person has a divinely created soul, and that all souls are equal before God. However, if we do not believe in the Christian myths about God, creation and souls, what does it mean that all people are "equal"?'[11]

Several Christian beliefs have led to this revolutionary way of thinking about human value.

1. We are created in God's image

Firstly, it is the conviction that humans have value because they are created. That idea comes right at the start of the Bible, in the book of Genesis, and is fundamental to us understanding who we are. We read:

> *So God created mankind in his own image,*
> *in the image of God he created them;*
> *male and female he created them.*[12]

Being created in the image of God does not, of course, mean that we physically look exactly like God. Rather, it means that something of what God is like is uniquely reflected in us as human beings. This sets us apart from anything else.

Therefore, the Christian conviction is that humans have value not because of what we *do*, but because of who we *are*. We are ultimately human *beings,* not human *doings!* Whatever our age, race, gender, sexuality, religion, intellect or ability, we *all* have value because we are created in the image of God.

This conviction has shaped so many of the great human rights achievements through history. It was clearly stated in the United States Declaration of Independence that 'all men are created equal'.[13] It was the firm belief of William Wilberforce, who, along with others, was instrumental in the abolition of the transatlantic slave trade. The Universal Declaration of Human Rights was massively influenced by the thinking of Charles Malik, the Lebanese diplomat, philosopher and theologian responsible for drafting it. The civil rights movement in the US was led by Martin Luther King, a Christian pastor who was also convinced that *all* people, no matter their race, have value because they are created in the image of God.

To see what Jesus himself thinks about this issue, let's go back to the story. Not only is the unconventional entry surprising, but so too is Jesus' response when these friends start destroying the roof of the house he is in. He does nothing!

Imagine you were in Jesus' shoes. When you realised people were destroying your friend's house just to reach you, what would you have done? I would have halted the proceedings immediately and either gone out to them, or asked others to leave to create room to let them in.

However, Jesus does neither. Instead, he simply lets them continue to destroy the ceiling – something that must have taken a few minutes, at least. Why?

I believe Jesus' passivity was actually a deliberate act of judgement on the other people in the house. He sees that they have no time or space for this disabled man, or for others like him. To them, this man means nothing. At best, they think he's unimportant; at worst, they think he's getting what he deserves. Jesus' response of allowing these friends to trash the house is effectively saying, 'This man may not mean much to you, but he does to me. In fact, he's worth more than your house. You may not have time or space for him, but I do.'

If you were to keep reading through Mark's account of Jesus' life, the very next event also shows how Jesus has time for people who no one else cared about.[14] He shows dignity and respect to those his society would have marginalised or despised. In fact, this is the repeated pattern of Jesus' life, and one that particularly riled the political and religious leaders of his day. One of their main criticisms of Jesus was that he had time for outsiders. What a great thing to be hated for! Although, of course, we only think that because the Jesus revolution has transformed the way we view the outsider and the weak.

Jesus shows us what it looks like to treat everybody as if they have infinite value and worth. Where his contemporaries discriminated on the basis of people's gender, ethnicity, religion or political affiliation, Jesus never did. He had time for women, teaching and talking with them, but never talking down to them. He commissioned them for significant tasks in his mission. He broke cultural barriers by going out of his way to speak to a Samaritan – a person from a religious and ethnic group that was despised by many of his contemporaries. His close group of followers included a Jewish zealot and a Roman tax collector – a bit like having a far-right politician and an Antifa activist among your best friends! Such radical inclusion was utterly counter-cultural and his example has shaped our world ever since.

Jesus' teaching and example consistently show how much he values each person – no matter who they are. Humans are worthy of human rights because we are created in the image of God. Yet experience tell us that sometimes human beings are capable of such awful acts that we doubt that we are worthy of anything. Jesus is not naïve to this destructive side to human nature, as we will now see.

The final surprise of the story is in what Jesus eventually said. Once the dust had settled and the man was lying in the middle of the room, you can imagine that everyone was waiting with bated breath for what Jesus would do next. The context of the story helps us to imagine what they were expecting. In the preceding account, we read of Jesus' unique ability to heal people with all kinds of serious ailments.[15] If Jesus was capable of such things, then surely they would have been expecting another miracle – for him to say, 'Get up and walk!' Instead, Jesus must have surprised everyone, not least the disabled man and his friends, when he simply declares, 'Son, your sins are forgiven.'

I can imagine the man looking up at Jesus and thinking, 'Wait a minute! That's not what I was after!'

In the same way, his friends would surely have thought, 'That's not why we destroyed this roof!'

Is Jesus unaware of this man's obvious need? No. In fact, he will go on to address it shortly. So why does he *start* with forgiveness? To everyone in the room, it seemed obvious that this man's great need was physical healing. However, by first addressing this man's sin, Jesus was actually pointing out a deeper problem – and not just with this man, but with each of us.

When we hear a word like 'sin', we are tempted to think simply of all the 'naughty but nice' things in life, like sex and chocolate. Yet when Jesus spoke of sin, he was describing a fundamental problem at the heart of humanity. Sin is that instinctive bias that we have to go the wrong way in life and to do the wrong thing. We have seen that Jesus treats all people with dignity and respect. He recognises that each of us has infinite value because of who we are before God. However, he also highlights that there is something fundamentally *broken* about each one of us.

Humanity is a paradox – we are capable of great acts of love, kindness and creativity, but we are also capable of destructive self-centredness that hurts others and destroys the world. It's not that some only do the former, while others only do the latter. *All* of us are capable of *both*. Are humans worthy of human rights? In one sense, yes – but in another sense, no!

Someone who deeply understood this view of humanity was the author C.S. Lewis. One of the characters in his Narnia Chronicles is a prince called Caspian. Aslan (the Jesus-like character in the stories) reveals to him that he comes from the same world from which the children have arrived in Narnia, and that, like them, he is human. 'You come from the Lord Adam and the Lady Eve,' said Aslan. 'And that is both honour enough to erect the head of the poorest beggar, and shame enough to bow the shoulders of the greatest emperor on earth. Be content.'[16]

Yet Jesus' purpose in speaking about the paralysed man's sin is not to condemn. In fact, it is quite the opposite. He has come to *forgive*. As the speaker and author J. John put it, 'Jesus didn't come to rub it in, but to rub it out!'[17] In the same breath, Jesus not only revealed what was wrong, but also claimed that he could put it right.

Jesus' audacious claim to be able to forgive is met with astonishment by some of those in the room. They rightly point out that forgiving sin is something that only God can do. But Jesus doesn't backtrack, clarify or change what he has said. Instead, he asks a question: what did they think was easier – to forgive sin or to heal paralysis?

On the one hand, it would seem that healing is much harder. Anyone can go around *claiming* to forgive sin – there's no objective way to know if it had actually happened. It's not like forgiven people suddenly change colour or start levitating six inches above the ground. By contrast, you'll soon know if someone can really heal or not. So to show that he can do the former, Jesus proceeds to do the latter.

Jesus doesn't just *say* the things that only God should say. He also *does* the things that only God can do. As we read on, we will see that he does this repeatedly, until things culminate with his ultimate claim – to be able to defeat death itself! (This is something we'll look at in chapter ten.)

2. In Jesus, God became one of us

For now, it is worth noting this: if Jesus' claim is true, it provides another reason as to why humanity is so significant. Not only are we created in the image of God (as Jewish people would also hold), but the uniquely *Christian* claim is that God also became one of us. God has permanently joined the human race, in the person of Jesus.

I was recently listening to a fascinating lecture by Professor John Wyatt,[18] a world expert in neonatology at University College Hospital in London who specialises in the care of extremely premature babies. He showed an incredible photo of an incident that took place while he was caring for one such baby. The baby suddenly reached out, their tiny but perfectly formed hand grasping one of John's fingers. John, himself a Christian, then asked the audience, 'Which hand do you think best represents the hand of God?'

Many would quickly assume that it is the much larger, stronger hand – rather like the one in the representation of God painted by Michelangelo on the ceiling of the Sistine Chapel. John, however, continued by suggesting that perhaps God is best represented by the baby's hand because the Christian conviction is that when Jesus was born, God became just as small and as vulnerable as that baby. He identifies with us in our fragility, in our weakness, in our poverty and in our oppression for he has experienced all of these. Each one of us is valuable not only because we are made in his image, but also because God himself became one of us.

3. In Jesus, God died for us

Furthermore, the Christian faith gives a third and even more significant reason for human value. To work this out, we need to think about Jesus' question again: 'Which is easier: to say to this paralysed man, "Your sins are forgiven," or to say, "Get up, take your mat and walk"?'[19] We assume that it is easier to forgive than to heal, but is it really? If we were to continue reading through this account of Jesus' life, we might realise that it is in fact the opposite.

For Jesus, to *heal* appeared to be relatively easy – it just took a word or a touch of his. In contrast, to *forgive* proved to be much more costly. We will discover that ultimately it cost Jesus his life. Forgiveness is always costly, as anyone who has had to forgive somebody who has hurt them can testify. We ourselves have to absorb the pain that we desire to pay back upon the other. In the same way, as Jesus died, he absorbed the ultimate pain … so that we might experience forgiveness.

The Christian faith says that God created us, became one of us and ultimately died for us. No other worldview or belief comes close to offering such a substantial basis for human rights.

2

Making sense
of our world

Where does our commitment to the environment come from?

When I was a student, anyone showing concern for environmental issues would have been treated with more than a little suspicion and deemed rather eccentric. Today, the opposite would be the case, and not without reason. We have become increasingly aware of the impact that our human behaviour has had on the planet.

Ever since the Industrial Revolution, we have witnessed a dramatic rise in global temperatures, setting off a chain reaction of destructive consequences. Sea levels are rising, habitats are being destroyed and whole species have become extinct. In the last fifty years, wildlife populations have decreased by 60%. One million plant, animal and insect species could become extinct this century. This impacts the whole human race, yet it is often the poorest who experience the worst consequences of the selfish consumption of the rich. The average UK resident consumes four times more of the earth's resources than the average Indian.[20] While the thought of warmer summers may seem an attractive proposition to a Brit, the increasing frequency of extreme weather patterns is bringing devastation to many other parts of the world, India included.

When we hear things like this, we instinctively feel that this is wrong. Very wrong! Yet maybe we haven't stopped to consider that this might be based not simply on our emotional gut reaction. Rather, is it rooted more deeply in the very nature of reality?

I remember travelling by train from the north of Romania to Budapest. Even when the train is running to time, this isn't a quick journey, and on this occasion it was running late! As we detoured around the branch lines of eastern Hungary, I got chatting to the guy sitting opposite and discovered that he was returning to university where he was studying environmental science.

I asked him what had motivated him to choose that particular course. He spoke animatedly about his deep concern for the environment and his desire to do something about our current crisis. I was impressed by his sincerity and his passion.

I then asked him, '*Why* do you think we should be concerned about the environment?'

He looked at me somewhat surprised and simply replied, 'Well, because we should!'

I agreed with him but asked again *why* he thought we should.

After a moment's reflection, he responded, 'Well, everyone knows we should.'

'But do they?' I asked. 'Surely if they did, then we wouldn't be in the mess we are in now? Surely the problem is that some people don't care about the environment?'

'Yes,' he responded, 'but they should!'

'But *why* should they?' I asked, yet again.

He thought for a moment and then admitted, 'I'm not sure I've ever really thought about that.'

I assured him that I wasn't trying to be clever. I was just trying to discuss on what basis we care for our world. If we are ever going to help those who disagree with us, we surely need to do more than simply making assertions. In addition, if we could better understand *why* we should care for the environment, then maybe we would also know *how* to motivate others to do so as well. If the greatest contributors to climate change are also (as often is the case) the least affected by it, then we need to think deeply about this question of motivation.

Getting rid of religion

One possible explanation for our concern for the environment is the decline of traditional religious beliefs. Religions are seen as being concerned with spiritual matters rather than the physical world. Religious salvation is seen as an escape from this physical world into another, more spiritual dimension. If that is the case, then what is the point of being concerned about this physical world now? In contrast, if this world is all we have, then we had better look after it!

The latter viewpoint argues that only as we are liberated from the baggage of traditional religions can we find a new concern for the environment. It is not so much that we are no longer religious, but that our religious beliefs have changed. Stop worrying about 'Father God' and show more concern for 'Mother Nature', some might say. Indeed, perhaps environmental concern has actually filled the void left by the decline of other religions and taken on a religious element of its own. Concern for the environment might give our lives a sense of meaning and purpose as we focus on something bigger than ourselves.

This identification of traditional religion as the problem certainly sounds like a plausible explanation when you consider a country like the United States. Their population has one the highest proportions of Christians in the world and yet they are also one of the biggest polluters. One American politician quipped, 'We don't need to look after the environment, the second coming of Christ is at hand.'[21] However, it is worth stopping to consider whether there is another way of looking at our concern for the environment.

A different perspective

While it may seem that religions offer little reason to be concerned for the environment, a closer look at the Christian faith reveals a different story. In fact, I would suggest that Christianity, far from seeing the environment as unimportant, gives us three great reasons to understand the huge importance of the physical world and therefore to be motivated to care for it.

1. God created the physical

Firstly, the Bible teaches that God made this physical world and declared that it was good. Human beings were created to enjoy the world as a gift but were also commanded to look after it. One of the first commands God gave humanity was to care for the world he had made.[22]

In the Old Testament part of the Bible, God gives more examples of what that might look like, including laws about sustainable farming and animal welfare. By creating human beings with unique dignity and value, God wasn't putting down the rest of his creation. Quite the opposite. Part of our uniqueness as humans is that we are to look after the rest of creation. This view of the world is quite different to that of other religions. For instance, Islam teaches that human beings only ended up on earth after they sinned against God. According to this belief, the world is not inherently good, but a place of judgement and testing.[23]

2. God became physical

Not only did God create the physical world, but the astonishing claim of Christianity is that he also became physical himself. The stunning declaration of the Christmas story is that God became human. Jim Irwin, the Apollo 15 astronaut, wrote, 'God walking on the earth is more important than man walking on the moon.'[24] By becoming human, God was affirming the original goodness of the world into which he came. He demonstrated that the physical world matters to him by becoming part of it.

Interestingly, this is the very reason why many Muslims explicitly reject the idea of Jesus being God. As they view the physical world as inherently evil, they struggle to believe that God could become a part of it. Indeed, many belief systems – both in classical antiquity and in modern-day Eastern religions – often perceive the physical world as something evil from which we need to be liberated. In contrast, Christians believe that God became physical, so have no problem affirming that the physical world is inherently good.

3. God will restore the physical

Of course, not everything about our world is good. There is much that is damaged and could be said to be broken. Yet, wonderfully, God's plan is not to destroy or discard this world and take us to some other dimension. Again, this is very different to other religions that view our ultimate destination as elsewhere.

According to the Bible, this physical world plays a central part in God's plans for the future and is indeed our true home! Ultimately, Christian salvation lies not in our removal from this world, but rather in the *renewal of* this world.[25] The Bible points forward to a day when God will restore everything!

Belief in action

One beautiful example of this biblical basis for environmental concern in action can be found in the north-west of Ethiopia and has been documented by Scottish photographer Kieran Dodds. In the last century, 90% of Ethiopia's forests have been lost to agriculture. Yet Ethiopia's Orthodox Tewahedo churches have developed a wonderful practice of actively stewarding the trees around their church buildings as a tenet of their faith, thus creating a network of 'green islands' in the midst of an otherwise arid landscape. The trees are seen as the clothes of the church. Kieran explains, 'The religious significance of the forest is equalled by its ecological function, impacting beneficially on ecosystems far beyond its walled boundary. These sacred oases raise water tables, cool temperatures, block destructive winds and are home to yield-boosting pollinators that are essential to surrounding agriculture.' His photos beautifully show the visible impact of these Christians' theological beliefs.[26]

To find out more about what Christians are doing in different parts of the world, do check out the work of A Rocha. This Christian charity supports communities in conservation work in every inhabited continent.[27]

In contrast to this, it is worth asking whether an atheistic belief really does give us such good motivation to care for the environment? We might say that if this world is all that we have, we had better look after it. However, if that is the case (and there is no God or spiritual dimension), then it is actually surprisingly hard to justify why we *should* look after it. Indeed, it is hard to explain why we should be morally obliged to do anything at all. If, as human beings, we are just the product of nature, then why should we be held morally responsible when we damage nature? We don't hold other animals morally responsible for what they do.

In his book *Sapiens,* the atheistic historian Yuval Noah Harari bemoans the way we have subjugated animals through mass farming.[28] Yet if we are just animals, who have advanced to our position through a process of evolution, then what is inherently wrong with this process? Surely we have just learnt to do more effectively (and on a larger scale) what other animals have been doing all the time?

Why the basis for our environmental concern matters

You might question what difference it makes that I believe that Christianity provides a more consistent and coherent reason for caring for the environment than other religions or atheism do. It is not *only* Christians who are deeply concerned for the environment; vast numbers have other beliefs or, like the student I met on the train, no religion at all. Shouldn't we just be happy that people care for the environment, whatever their beliefs?

However, I'm convinced that Christianity doesn't simply best explain *why* we should care for the environment. It also fundamentally affects *how* we should think about environmental concerns today, and how we might respond to the challenge.

I was chatting to a local politician recently who revealed that, while they are concerned about environmental issues, they are also deeply concerned about some of the ways that this cause has been promoted. They are not alone. Indeed, I would suggest that serious environmental concern divorced from a Christian worldview will ultimately lead to a sense of disillusionment and despair, as we increasingly realise the magnitude and seeming impossibility of the task to which we are called. I believe that Christianity should make us *more pessimistic* about the problem ... and yet also *more hopeful* about the solution.

The problem

I was standing on an underground platform in London when I first noticed a huge billboard proclaiming, 'Technology will save us'.[29] It summed up well how many people believe we can solve the current environmental challenges, but is technology really the answer?

I was struck by this admission from Gus Speth, an American environmental lawyer and advocate:

> *I used to think that the top environmental problems were biodiversity loss, ecosystem collapse and climate change. I thought that thirty years of good science could address these problems. I was wrong. The top environmental problems are selfishness, greed and apathy, and to deal with these we need a cultural and spiritual transformation.*[30]

Humanity's problem is not that we don't know something needs to be done. Nor is it even that we aren't sure what we could do. Our problem is that often we simply don't do it. It is all too easy to say the right things and yet still not *do* anything. This might be simply down to our apathy, or maybe it is because actually *doing* something can be costly – individually and corporately. Especially in the West, where we are shielded from some of the more devastating implications of climate change, we can easily be unconcerned and unmoved.

We have already seen how, in the Bible, one of the key responsibilities God gives to people is to care for the world. Our failure to do just that shows we are out of step with the God who made us. Instead of loving God, loving others and loving his world as the Bible commands us, we have often loved ourselves and our own comfort most of all.

Our need, therefore, is not simply for better technology or more information, but for a radical change of heart in each one of us. Indeed, if the problem lies in the human heart, then technology (which is created by flawed human beings) can never be relied on to sort out the problem. Wonderfully, however, the Christian faith is all about how we can be reconnected to the God from whom we have alienated ourselves. The centre of the Christian faith is about how our hearts can be transformed by the kindness and forgiveness of Jesus. Becoming a Christian doesn't just change the way we think about God; it also changes the way we think about his world.

An illustration might help to show how being reconnected to God makes a difference to the way we view the world. I have only ever driven two BMWs. The first was a rental car that I picked up in Turkey a few years ago when I got fed up with relying upon very unpredictable public transport (and my non-existent Turkish!) to get around. You should understand that I hadn't ordered such a fancy car. I always order the smallest, cheapest vehicle. However, as I have discovered so often happens, the cheapest car wasn't available on that day. So when they asked if I would mind having to drive a BMW X1 instead, I explained that I would have to put up with that if it was all that was available! I certainly enjoyed making full use of its superior capabilities!

The second time I drove a BMW was when our own car was delayed during its annual service at the garage. As we had to go out, our very kind neighbour lent us his car for the evening. Was there a difference to how I drove that compared to the hire car? Of course!

It was Jeremy Clarkson who once pointed out that the fastest car in the world is a hire car. When I drove the hire car, my relationship to the owner was purely legal. As long as I didn't scratch it, it didn't really matter how I drove it. When I borrowed my neighbour's car, my relationship to the owner was personal. It changed the way I used it.

Many people have a realisation that this world doesn't belong to us. They might even believe that there is some kind of deity behind the whole universe. However, being a Christian means that we *know* that God personally, and the way we treat his stuff reveals what we think of him. For a Christian, caring for the environment is not simply an act of obedience to a command; it is also an act of love towards God himself. Christianity addresses the root problem behind the environmental problems of our world – human greed and selfishness – and offers a solution.

The solution

While Christianity may make us more pessimistic about human nature than other viewpoints, it will also lead us to a greater hope for the future.

I have noticed that some who campaign about environmental issues are often driven by a great sense of fear of the future. The very name Extinction Rebellion reveals this. In some ways, this fear is completely understandable, considering how bad the state of our world is. But there are a number of dangers in trying to motivate people through fear.

Fear overstates the case

Firstly, there is a temptation to overstate the case for something in an effort to make ourselves heard, which can ultimately undermine the case when people stop to question our claims. For instance, when Greta Thunberg claimed that within ten years humans could be on the verge of becoming extinct,[31] it caused many to feel the urgency of the situation. But it would appear that most climate scientists, while concerned for the environment, don't share such an extreme outlook.

Fear causes anxiety

Secondly, there is a danger that fear creates unhealthy levels of anxiety – particularly in young people. Telling schoolchildren that they might be wiped out in a few years could hardly be helpful to those of a generation which, studies have shown, experiences higher levels of anxiety than any before it. Could environmental fears be one of the contributing factors?[32]

Fear leads to ill-thought-through responses

Another potential problem with being motivated by fear is that it can lead to knee-jerk reactions that aren't always well-thought-through. Overwhelmed by the scale of the problem, we sense that we 'need to do something', but don't always stop to think through the effectiveness of those actions.

This was highlighted when the Formula One driver Lewis Hamilton took to Instagram to share his fears for the future of our world. He wrote, 'Extinction of our race becoming more and more likely as we overuse our resources. The world is a messed-up place. World leaders either uneducated or don't care about the environment at all.' While his concern was admirable, his proposed solution caused some consternation: 'Go Vegan. It is the only way to truly save our planet today.'[33] A number of commentators pointed out the irony that a man who makes his living flying around the world driving gas-guzzling cars is unable to think of any other way of saving the world than giving up meat!

There is a danger that we come up with simplistic solutions without thinking through their implications. Yes, chopping down rainforests to rear cattle for beef is terrible for the environment, but so too is clearing forests to grow avocados that then need to be flown around the world to be smashed on my toast in a trendy café! This doesn't mean that what we eat doesn't matter – our diet *can* make a difference. But no solution is as simple as just giving up meat and dairy.

Fear produces despair

A further problem with motivating people by fear is that, instead of mobilising them to act, it can actually lead them to despair. When we exclusively emphasise the way that humanity has destroyed the world, we might cause people to think that humanity itself is merely a problem to be eliminated.

If we view humanity as nothing more than a plague, then one obvious solution to the environmental crisis is to have less people in the world. On one level, this can be seen in the increasingly popular decision not to have children in order to reduce future CO_2 emissions. Yet, taken to extremes, the same thinking could also lead people to decide to remove themselves from the world through suicide. It could even cause people to want to remove others at the same time. It is interesting that a number of mass killers have expressed utter despair not simply at themselves but at humanity in general.

Humans have the ability to do good!

It is true that locusts may destroy crops and beavers damage river habitats, but nothing has the unique capability of destroying our world like humanity has. Yet it is also true that we have unique ability to do *good* for our world. In their bestselling book on climate change, *Small Gases, Big Effect,* German students David Nelles and Christian Serrer explain that the fact that humans are directly responsible for climate change is 'ironically … good news: it's a reminder that we can influence how our climate develops in the future. We are not powerless against climate change.'[34]

Perhaps our problem is that we too easily see the destructive impact of humanity on our world, but at the same time can be blinkered to the way we can constructively tend and care for it. An example of this is how we might respond when we go for a walk in the countryside. We might feel that we are getting away from the impact of humanity (skyscrapers and factories) to see pure, unblemished nature (fields and hedgerows and cows and sheep). What we can so easily forget is that the beautiful countryside views are not only God's creation, but also the product of what humanity can accomplish. Without human intervention, there would be no fields or hedgerows! While farming methods can sometimes be destructive to the environment, when done properly, they can have a positive effect on the landscape and the environment.

I am writing this chapter looking out on St Ives Bay from the holiday home where we are staying in Cornwall,

England. In the distance, the waves of an autumn storm are smashing against the rocks beneath Godrevy Lighthouse, while a vivid rainbow arcs across the sky, plunging into the sea behind it. It's breathtaking, but what makes the view even more beautiful is what I can see in the foreground. A gorgeous garden stretches out in front of the house to the dunes beyond. Cape daisies dance in the late-afternoon sunlight while ornamental grasses blow in the wind. Yet this didn't happen by itself. Gardens need to be planted, tended and watered. The view in front of me has been enhanced by what humans have done.

Jesus will restore the whole of creation!

Humanity has unique power – for good and ill. As a Christian, this doesn't surprise me because the Bible says human beings were created with a unique responsibility to care for our world. It is interesting that the whole biblical account begins with people being placed in a garden, the Garden of Eden – a place that requires continual human involvement. The very first job given to humanity is gardening!

This idea of gardening comes up again later in the Bible. Three days after Jesus' crucifixion, Mary, one of his followers, has heard reports that the tomb where his body had been placed has been found empty. She runs to the tomb to look for herself and, as expected, finds that the body is no longer there.

With tears in her eyes, she turns away from the tomb and sees someone standing in the garden. Blinded by her tears, she fails to see that it is in fact Jesus, alive again. He asks her, 'Why are you crying? Who is it you are looking for?' Mary assumes the man must be the gardener, so says, 'Sir, if you have carried him away, tell me where you have put him, and I will get him.' Jesus responds by simply calling her name – 'Mary'. We then read:

> She turned towards him and cried out in Aramaic, 'Rabboni!' (which means 'Teacher').
>
> Jesus said, 'Do not hold on to me, for I have not yet ascended to the Father. Go instead to my brothers and tell them, 'I am ascending to my Father and your Father, to my God and your God.'
>
> Mary Magdalene went to the disciples with the news: 'I have seen the Lord!' And she told them that he had said these things to her.[35]

When Mary first sees Jesus, her initial response is to mistake him for a gardener. On one level, this is an understandable mistake. They were in a garden – the kind of place where you might expect a gardener to be! Also, Mary, like the other followers of Jesus, was not expecting Jesus to rise from the dead. In her mind, the possibility of meeting a gardener was far higher than meeting her friend who had just been horrifically executed. In fact, despite Jesus' repeated predictions of his death and resurrection, the first reaction of all the disciples to the evidence of the resurrection is incredulity. This is helpful to remember. The reason the early Christians came to believe in the resurrection was not that they were more inclined to believe such a claim – you don't need a degree in biology to know that dead people normally stay dead! Rather, they believed because they became convinced by the evidence. (We will think more about this in chapter ten.)

Mary mistaking Jesus for a gardener is significant, though, in terms of the whole Bible story. The first human being in the Bible was created to be a gardener – to tend and care for the world that God had made. That human gardener failed at his job, as humanity has so often ever since. However, Jesus rises to life as the representative of a new humanity, and the first person he is mistaken for is a gardener! As the ultimate 'head gardener', he is going to restore all that is broken – not just in us, but in all of creation. Indeed, the Bible finishes by painting a picture of the future of our world as a garden city.[36]

Jesus' resurrection doesn't just tell us that we can somehow survive death, but that one day everything will be restored. The resurrection promise is that one day the whole of creation will be transformed and renewed. Therefore, Christians look to the future not with despair, but with hope. While humanity has often damaged so much of what is good in the world, Jesus, the true human, has come to restore what is broken. Furthermore, just as he calls Mary by name, he invites us personally to join him in his garden. As friends of the head gardener, we can partner with him in caring for his world and look forward in hope to the day when everything will be restored.

I admire the 'stubborn optimism' of environmental campaigners like the Costa Rican diplomat Christiana Figueres. She admits that we may not win, but states we must still fight.[37] However, I believe that Jesus gives us confidence that we're not fighting a losing battle. We *will* win. Christianity invites us to be motivated not by despair, but by hope.

I love the motto of A Rocha, the Christian environmental organisation that I mentioned earlier: 'Conservation and hope'. Their website is filled with stories of hope that show what can positively be done to make a real difference. For example, one forest in Kenya was being destroyed by locals, who were cutting it down to rear and then sell animals for meat. A Rocha discovered this was because they needed money to pay for their children's schooling. Working with the community, they set up an ecotourism programme that provided scholarships and employment. Now, the community is invested in preserving their precious ecosystem and everyone is better off as a result.[38]

Personally, I have found the Bible's teaching such a great encouragement and motivation in my own life. Sometimes, I have felt overwhelmed at the scale of the problem facing humanity and have struggled to see how my seemingly small actions can have any real impact. Will leaving my car at home, using my reusable cup and shopping bags, and eating locally produced meat and veg really stop the 141 billion tonnes of ice being lost from Antarctica every year? Surely it is global superpowers that can have the biggest impact, and I have little say on their choices? My small and seemingly insignificant actions all seem too little, too late. But then I remember that they are not insignificant to God. They can be worked as an act of love for him. Nor are they fruitless, for I know that far from fighting a losing battle, the Christian story tells me that, one day, this battle will be won!

3

Making sense of happiness

Is there more to life than being happy?

It may seem rather strange that I am writing about happiness. Surely there are better qualified people to speak about the topic? For a start, I'm British, and we Brits aren't exactly known for our sunny demeanour. We are more used to keeping calm and carrying on!

According to Eric Weiner, author of *The Geography of Bliss*, Brits really don't know much about happiness. 'I feel sorry for the Brits,' he writes. 'The Brits don't merely enjoy misery, they get off on it … in Britain the happy are few and suspect. Britain is a great place for grumps, and most Brits, I suspect, derive a perverse pleasure from their grumpiness.'[39]

Weiner spent a year travelling the world. He wanted to know not so much *who* was happy, but *where* people were happy. It was the residents of the UK who were recipients of his greatest feelings of sympathy. Indeed, one town stood out for particular criticism. 'Slough,' he proclaimed, 'is a treasure trove of unhappiness, buried beneath a copious layer of gloom. The colours range from deeper to lighter shades of grey. The people seem grey too and slightly dishevelled.'[40] I should probably come clean and admit that I did indeed live within the postcode of Slough – though, I hasten to add, not within the town itself!

According to the UN-commissioned World Happiness Report,[41] if you want to know about happiness, then you should head north. It is the Nordic countries that regularly top the league table of happiness.

There is a second reason why some would deem me ill-qualified to speak about happiness: I am a Christian. Surely the demands of religious observance are at odds with desiring happiness? Isn't religion about supressing our desire for happiness in pursuit of some more virtuous and future goal? People become religious for many reasons but, most people would assume, it is not normally out of a desire for happiness.

I laughed when I saw one church billboard proclaim, 'Why be depressed alone? Come inside and join us!' I am not sure they intended the meaning that many people would have taken from it!

We may not ordinarily associate happiness with religiosity. However, studies show that the things that we often do associate with happiness are surprisingly ineffective in bringing it about.

Happiness is hard to find

Affluenza[42] is a fascinating book by the British clinical psychologist Oliver James. In it, he makes a compelling argument that, unless you are living in extreme poverty, increasing affluence is not correlated to increasing happiness. Indeed, the opposite seems to be the case. He describes much of the West as being infected with a pandemic of affluenza – a relentless desire to accumulate more in order to keep pace with those around us. This only leads to greater levels of anxiety and depression. Beyond a certain level, happiness is often inversely proportional to how much we own.

Another fascinating insight into the subject of happiness comes from the American social psychologist Jonathan Haidt. In his book *The Happiness Hypothesis*,[43] he reveals that, while many of us believe that a change in our life circumstances will make us happy, studies show that life changes have minimal long-term impact upon our actual levels of happiness. He proves this by comparing the emotional states of those who have a sudden improvement in their circumstances, such as people who win the lottery, with those who have a sudden deterioration, like those who become paralysed in a car accident.

Unsurprisingly, those who win the lottery report an immediate improvement in their emotional state, while those who become paralysed experience the opposite. What is surprising, though, is that within a year, the happiness levels of both sets of people have normally returned to where they were before things changed. Those who won the lottery have become used to their new situation, while those who were paralysed have often learnt to adapt to a new way of living. In other words, changes in life circumstances may make us happy or sad in the short term, but they have very little power to bring us lasting happiness.

Yet another insight into happiness comes from Tal Ben-Shahar. For many years, he taught one of the most popular classes at Harvard. It was on the subject of happiness. In his book *Happier*,[44] he outlines two ways that many people pursue happiness. The first is that of the hedonist, who simply does whatever gives maximum pleasure in the moment, regardless of the long-term consequences. It is not hard to see the problem with such an approach. Equally problematic is the second method, which he calls the 'rat race' view of happiness. These are people who identify happiness with some future event, forgoing immediate pleasure to pursue that long-term goal. The problem is that once that goal has been attained, while they may feel a sense of relief, they don't really experience lasting happiness.

Jim Carrey, one of the most successful actors of the last thirty years, summed this up well when he said, 'I think everybody should get rich and famous and do everything they ever dreamed of so they can see that it's not the answer.'[45] The hope of lasting happiness can turn out to be little more than a mirage on the horizon. We believe that it's within our reach, but we never quite get there.

Tal Ben-Shahar explains that to find real happiness, we need to be able to enjoy the moment while also having a long-term goal to work towards: 'Attaining lasting happiness requires that we enjoy the journey on our way toward a destination we deem valuable. Happiness is not about making it to the peak of the mountain nor is it about climbing aimlessly around the mountain; happiness is the experience of climbing toward the peak.'[46]

I came to realise this myself a number of years ago on one of my own journeys. Inspired by the heroic tale of a man who cycled through a Siberian winter (which I read in the comfort of my warm bed), I decided I needed to go on my own adventure. So I set out to cycle the length of Great Britain between its most south-westerly and north-easterly points. It wasn't quite as heroic as cycling through Siberia, but given that until that point I'd never cycled more than thirty miles and I had done no prior training, it turned out to be quite an ordeal.[47]

I remember lying in my tent one morning in the Scottish Highlands, listening to the rain and aching from the previous day's cycling. The thought of getting out of my warm sleeping bag and back onto my bike was not a pleasant one. If I had listened to my feelings in that moment, I would have stayed in bed. Or maybe I would have got on a train home, flown to somewhere sunny and sat on a beach.

Thankfully, I chose to ignore those feelings, and pressed on through a headwind and rain. Within a couple of hours, the rain started to ease and the sun came out. I found myself cycling through a sunlit glen as a rainbow was arcing across the distant mountains. I was so overwhelmed at the sense of joy and wonder in the moment that I found myself in tears as I pedalled onwards.

Having an end goal gave me a sense of purpose, which kept me going through the hard times. However, I was also able to enjoy some incredible moments en route, rather than simply waiting for the end. That turned out to be just as well, as I discovered that John O' Groats (the most north-easterly town on mainland Britain) is one of the most underwhelming places I have ever been!

All of these authors discussed above offer real wisdom on the subject, but it could be that there is a more fundamental problem with our search for happiness: we are starting with the wrong question. All too often we begin by asking, 'What will make me happy?' Perhaps, though, we need to consider whether there is more to life than just being happy. Do many of our problems with achieving happiness come from the fact that we have mistakenly made it our greatest aim in life?

Making happiness our goal in life is problematic

In his book *Sapiens*, Yuval Noah Harari agrees that many of the things that we think will make us happy will actually fail: 'Money, social status, plastic surgery, beautiful houses, powerful positions – none of these will bring you happiness.' But his conclusion may be surprising to some:

'Lasting happiness only comes from serotonin, dopamine and oxytocin.'[48]

If happiness is nothing more than the release of chemicals in our brain, and such an emotion can be replicated through drugs, then perhaps this should make us question whether we ultimately want happiness. Could happiness be too small and superficial an aim in life? Perhaps there is more to life than just being happy?

Someone who also deals with this topic is the Canadian psychologist Jordan Peterson.[49] In his thought-provoking book *12 Rules for Life,* his seventh rule is: 'Pursue what is meaningful (not what is expedient).'[50] It is interesting that when we look at the lives of others, those who pursue the former tend to gain our respect and admiration far more than the latter.

As I was writing this chapter, I became distracted and started scrolling through Twitter. A great deal of the discussion that day seemed to centre around the actions of two celebrities. One had taken her friends to a private island for a holiday; the other had been spearheading a campaign to help feed poor schoolchildren. Interestingly, the first was regarded with derision while the second was admired as a hero. Undoubtedly, an island holiday was probably better at producing temporal feelings of happiness than mashing potatoes, but we seem to instantly recognise that there is something more meaningful and lasting about the actions of the second.

If you're still not convinced, then think of how different some of the best-loved stories would have been if their main characters' chief aim was their own personal happiness. Would Frodo have ever taken the ring to Mordor, or would he have stayed in the Shire enjoying his three breakfasts a day? Would the children in Narnia have confronted the White Witch in battle, or beaten a hasty retreat to England through the wardrobe? Would Batman have returned to Gotham City? Would Clark Kent have left Lois Lane to answer the cries for Superman? Would Luke Skywalker have ever left his island hideaway?

In fact, pursuing immediate happiness is not only superficial, but also means that we have no means of developing ways of coping with suffering and hardship in life. Indeed, Western society's struggle to come to terms with the reality of suffering betrays our faulty philosophy of happiness.

Suffering is, of course, a universal reality; it affects all people. Yet it doesn't affect all people the same. The irony in the West is that while, relatively speaking, we could be said to suffer far less than others, we seem to struggle with suffering the most. Let me explain what I mean.

There has probably never been a generation or culture in history that has actually experienced *less* suffering than today's Western society. While we experience real suffering, we (on the whole) suffer far less compared to previous generations and to other parts of the world. For instance, I know a couple of friends who have lost a child in infancy. They have experienced great tragedy. Yet one hundred years ago, virtually every parent would have lost at least one child. Indeed, infant mortality remains high in other parts of the world – one in ten children in Afghanistan never reach their fifth birthday.

The Covid-19 pandemic has had a huge impact upon our world, and we have been graphically told daily the number of people who have died. Again, each death has been a tragedy. However, once figures are adjusted to take into account today's increased population, the number of deaths has actually been thousands of times lower than it was during the Spanish Flu pandemic of 1918. Our relative wealth in the West also ensured that we were insulated from some of the worst collateral damage of the pandemic in ways that other parts of the world could not afford.

Secular thinkers, including the cognitive psychologist Stephen Pinker and the historian Yuval Noah Harari, likewise point out that in many ways life, especially in the West, is better than it has ever been.

Yet, as I previously said, while today's Western society actually seems to suffer less than other cultures and generations, we appear to struggle more with the question of suffering. I have travelled widely across the world giving talks about the Christian faith. In doing so, I have sought to be open to whatever questions people have. I am struck that while the most common question in the West is almost always about suffering, this comes up far less frequently in other parts of the world. Why might those who suffer the *least* struggle with it the *most*? I would suggest that the problem is not the magnitude of our suffering, but our belief about life.

If I believe that my purpose in life is to be happy, then I will always struggle with suffering for it will always stop me from achieving my purpose. However, if I could find something bigger to live for than my own personal, immediate happiness, could suffering, in some way, serve towards that greater purpose?

The search for meaning and satisfaction

Jonathan Haidt suggests in *The Happiness Hypothesis* that we can gain much wisdom by going back to some of the great thinkers of the past.[51] One such person he looks at is Jesus. So as Haidt suggests, let's see how Jesus speaks into this subject when he encounters someone who, by many people's reckoning, should have had everything he needed to be happy.

As Jesus started on his way, a man ran up to him and fell on his knees before him. 'Good teacher,' he asked, 'what must I do to inherit eternal life?'

'Why do you call me good?' Jesus answered. 'No one is good – except God alone. You know the commandments: "You shall not murder, you shall not commit adultery, you shall not steal, you shall not give false testimony, you shall not defraud, honour your father and mother."'

'Teacher,' he declared, 'all these I have kept since I was a boy.'

Jesus looked at him and loved him. 'One thing you lack,' he said. 'Go, sell everything you have and give to the poor, and you will have treasure in heaven. Then come, follow me.'

At this the man's face fell. He went away sad, because he had great wealth.[52]

This encounter is recorded in all three of the earliest biographies of Jesus' life. Piecing them together, we discover that the man in question was not only rich, but also young and held a position of influence in the local community. In some ways, this man had everything that people want – wealth, youth and power.

Why should such a person be interested in what Jesus has to offer? Surely he already has everything he desires? However, perhaps that's exactly the point. Sometimes, it's only when you have everything you want that you realise that it is not everything you need.

Chris Boardman achieved remarkable success as a cyclist, becoming Britain's first Olympic champion in the sport for seventy-two years. Yet after dedicating so much to the achievement of this success, he reflected:

Your entire life is wrapped up in getting this one thing. You believe this one thing is the answer. Once you've got this one thing, you tell yourself, you'll be satisfied. The lucky ones get there and find that it isn't the answer, then they go looking in the right places for satisfaction and happiness. It's not wrapped up in a gold medal.[53]

In a sense, this man who encounters Jesus is lucky: he has realised his dreams while still young and therefore has come to realise relatively early that there must be more to life. How sad to spend your whole life pursuing a dream, only to discover too late that it would never be fulfilling.

Not only is the man interested in Jesus, but it also seems rather odd that he comes asking about eternal life. Isn't he a bit young to be worrying about what happens when you die? Yet there are two reasons why this is not as strange as we might think.

Firstly, as Tal Ben-Shahar points out, to know happiness in the present, we need to have some future goal or purpose in our life. It is not enough simply to enjoy the journey; we need to know where the journey is heading. This makes it important to think about life's destination, even if we feel that is still a long way off. Of course, though, if death is the end – for me, for you and for the universe – then the journey doesn't ultimately have a destination. The more we think about that, the more it robs us of happiness now.

Secondly, we need to understand what the words 'eternal life' mean in the context of the Bible. We might immediately assume that they simply refer to what happens after you die. But according to the Bible, eternal life is also something that you could experience now. It is the life of the age to come, which is available in the present. It is not merely about a *quantity* of life, but also about a *quality* of life. It is not just about life *after* death; it's also about life *before* death. So by enquiring about eternal life, this man is not simply asking about the future; he is also asking what makes life meaningful in the present. Once more, Tal Ben-Shahar helps us here by explaining that it is not enough simply to pin our hopes on reaching our final destination. We need to be able to enjoy the journey on the way there.[54]

Elsewhere, Jesus defined exactly what he meant by the eternal life he offers: 'Now this is eternal life: that they know you, the only true God, and Jesus Christ, whom you have sent.'[55] Eternal life means knowing God. 'Knowing', in this context, doesn't simply refer to some intellectual knowledge that you accumulate, like you would to pass an exam. Rather, it is the knowledge that comes from a personal and intimate relationship. (In fact, in the Bible, 'knowing someone' was a euphemism used to describe the act of sex.)

Eternal life is therefore about coming to know a deep, personal, lasting, fruitful connection with the God who made you, and who is revealed to you in Jesus. Far from taking away that which makes life worth living, Jesus says, 'I have come that they may have life, and have it to the full.'[56]

Speaking of this desire for real life, the author C.S. Lewis explains that often our problem is not that we want too much, but that we settle for too little:

If we consider the unblushing promises of reward … promised in the Gospels, it would seem that our Lord finds our desires not too strong, but too weak. We are half-

hearted creatures, fooling about with drink and sex and ambition when infinite joy is offered us, like an ignorant child who wants to go on making mud pies in a slum because he cannot imagine what is meant by the offer of a holiday at the sea. We are far too easily pleased.[57]

How do we get this life? Jesus' response to the man's question is a little surprising. In true rabbinical fashion, he responds to the question with a question of his own: 'Why do you call me good? ... No one is good – except God alone.'[58]

Why does Jesus ask him that? This young man has just enquired what he needs to *do* to get eternal life. Behind his question is an assumption that there is something that you can *do* to make yourself good enough to deserve such life. Jesus blows that assumption out of the water, effectively saying, 'You think there is something you can do to make yourself good enough. But only God is good enough. And your application to join the Godhead has just been rejected!'

Jesus next goes on to list a number of the commandments from the first part of the Bible, such as not murdering, stealing or lying. The young man responds by assuring Jesus that he has kept them all. Jesus responds by telling the young man that there is something he can do – he can sell all he has and give to the poor.

Does this mean, then, that the only way to eternal life is found in selling your possessions? Is this a universal command? The Bible certainly does encourage generous giving, but I don't think this request to give away everything is intended for everyone wanting to become a Christian. For a start, some people have little or nothing to give away. What is more, if this were a universal command, there would, in theory, be one person in the world who couldn't become a Christian because they would now own everything that everyone else had given away!

Jesus' command does, though, reveal the problem in this man's heart, and indeed the problem that we all have. When Jesus listed the Ten Commandments, he only referred to the last seven that deal with our attitude towards other people. He left out the first three that deal with our attitude towards God. This man would have known that those very first commands are about not having any other gods before God.

In telling this man to give away all that he has, Jesus is actually revealing that the man has another god in his life – his money. The tragedy of this story is that while the man already knows that his money cannot satisfy him, he still can't give it up to gain what really will be satisfying. He wants the life that Jesus can give him, but *in addition to*, rather than instead of, the things that he already has.

This is often how we are tempted to think about God. We might like the idea that Jesus could add something to our lives – in the way that air conditioning might be an added benefit to your car. But the change that Jesus is talking about is more fundamental. He is not to be a bolt-on extra to life, but its very foundation. This involves a radical reorientation of our whole lives.

The man leaves sad because he is unwilling to do such a huge task. He wants life, but Jesus' request seems like the end of life. Yet this is the counterintuitive nature of Christianity.

Counterintuitive Christianity

Shortly before this incident, Jesus had said: '… whoever wants to save their life will lose it, but whoever loses their life for me and for the gospel will save it. What good is it for someone to gain the whole world, yet forfeit their soul?'[59] In other words, Jesus was stating that the only way to get real life is to give your life away. The only way to discover true happiness is to stop making that your goal, and instead to make something, or rather some*one*, else your goal.

How can Jesus make such demands? And why should we believe that they will guarantee human flourishing?[60]

The incident we have been looking at is sometimes referred to by Bible commentators as the story of the 'Rich, Young Ruler', and for obvious reasons. But on closer inspection, it is actually the story of the 'Rich, Young Ruler*s'* because Jesus was also all of these things. Not only was he young, but, as God incarnate, he rightly owned and ruled everything there was. He was the ultimate 'Rich, Young Ruler'. Yet the story of Jesus' rule is so different. He didn't cling hold of what he had, but incredibly gave it away – *for us*. Speaking of Jesus, one early Christian wrote, 'though he was rich, yet for your sake he became poor, so that you through his poverty might become rich'.[61]

The story of the Bible is of a God who gave up everything out of love for us. When we start to understand that, we begin to realise that it might be worth giving up everything for him. In doing so, we don't really lose *anything*, but rather gain *everything*.

C.S. Lewis, whom I mentioned earlier, was not always a believer. Indeed, for much of his life, he was an atheist. He was helped on his journey to faith through his close friendship with fellow author J.R.R Tolkien. Lewis had many objections to the Christian faith and really didn't want it to be true. Yet one night, after a long walk with his friend, Lewis came to a realisation that he could run from God no longer. He wrote:

> *You must picture me alone in that room in Magdalen, night after night, feeling, whenever my mind lifted even for a second from my work, the steady, unrelenting approach of Him whom I so earnestly desired not to meet. That which I greatly feared had at last come upon me. In the Trinity Term of 1929 I gave in, and admitted that God was God, and knelt and prayed: perhaps, that night, the most dejected and reluctant convert in all England.[62]*

Lewis took this step so reluctantly because he felt that it would, in some ways, be the end of life. He feared what becoming a Christian would mean. Yet what he discovered was quite the opposite of what he expected, hence the title of his semi-autobiographical work: *Surprised by Joy*. In it, he recounts not only meeting his wife (who was called Joy), but also how he was surprised to find deep and meaningful joy in Jesus.

If our goal in life is to seek happiness, then we will find, like a mirage, that it will evade us. However, if we make it our aim to know Jesus, and to give up our selfish life to follow him and serve others, then we may just find something deeper than temporal happiness – we may discover true and lasting joy. This is what Lewis meant when he concluded, 'Aim at Heaven and you will get Earth "thrown in": aim at Earth and you will get neither.'[63]

Christianity isn't simply about discovering the small beer of happiness, but about finding the truly potent, stronger stuff of joy. Happiness is temporal and dependent on favourable life events. In contrast, real joy is lasting and can be discovered in spite of, and indeed even because of, the difficulties in life that we may go through.

4

Making sense
of society

How can we find peace in an increasingly polarised world?

I recently made the mistake of asking a question about a political issue on social media. One week and many angry comments later, I was starting to wish I hadn't! The hostility and animosity in the resulting interactions were remarkable.

My experience is not uncommon. Many have noted how Western society has become increasingly polarised. It's not that people never disagreed before, but that the hostility with which debates now rage seems unprecedented.

Battles are fought over a whole variety of issues. Brexit, American presidential elections, LGBT rights, police killings, coronavirus restrictions and environmental policies have all led to real hostility between those of opposing views. This battle is not only fought with words on social media, but at times has spilled over into actual violence in our cities and on our university campuses.[64]

This growing problem has been noticed by those on both sides of the political divide. Douglas Murray is a conservative British commentator who examines these worrying trends in his bestselling book *The Madness of Crowds*.[65] At the same time, the American psychologist Jonathan Haidt (himself left-leaning, politically) focuses on this in his excellent book *The Coddling of the American Mind*[66] that he co-authored with lawyer and writer Greg Lukianoff. In it, they offer an insightful critique of what is happening in Western society. Political journalist Ian Dunt agrees that the problem is not limited to those of just one political persuasion. He writes that we need to 'accept that both left and right have a problem. Far too many on either side claim that their tribe is blameless while the other is pernicious. No reasonable assessment of what we see online corresponds with that narrative.'[67]

Indeed, such has been the shift in our society that a whole new vocabulary has developed to describe what is going on. If we don't like someone's views, then instead of just ignoring them, we can *call them out*, or campaign to have them *no-platformed*. We can ensure that they are *publicly shamed* or even *cancelled*.[68]

Those who show concern about social justice issues can get labelled *Marxist*. Being passionate about environmental issues can get you mocked as an *eco-warrior*. Sharing your experience of racism can be dismissed as *playing the race card*. Campaigning for women's rights can lead to you being rejected as a *feminazi*. All of this has prompted a growing number of people to start raising concerns about where it might be heading.[69]

I experienced something of this first-hand when I was no-platformed by a university in Denmark, another in Finland and then narrowly avoided the same fate in a British university a couple of years later. On none of these occasions could the university authorities point to anything I had ever said or done that led to their decision. Instead, it seemed to be more a fear of what I *might* say, given my Christian belief.

How did the situation become like this? How did we end up so polarised?

The role of social media

One potential factor for this polarisation has been the increasing use of social media. It is very easy to surround ourselves online with people who share the same views as ourselves, and block those who don't. Indeed, social media algorithms positively encourage this isolationism by showing us what they think that we may already like. We end up constructing what has become popularly known as an *echo chamber*, where we hear our own ideas repeated back to us through the posts of others. This only serves to reinforce our views, while making the thought of anyone disagreeing with us seem all the more absurd.

This came home to me with one comment I noticed on Twitter just before a recent election in the UK. When it emerged that the Conservative Party had a significant lead in the polls, one person bemoaned, 'How is this even possible?! I don't even know any f***ing Tories!' Despite the fact that the poll (and the subsequent election) clearly revealed that a good deal of the population shared at least some of the Conservative Party's views, this person had clearly constructed a world where they never encountered any of them.

Another problem with communication online is that it can embolden us to say things that we would never actually say to someone's face. It changes us. This is a particular issue in my own country. In her humorous and insightful book about British culture, *Watching the English*,[70] Kate Fox notes how Brits typically hate disagreeing with each other about anything. We feel compelled to endorse other people's views even when we think they are clearly wrong – even when the topic is as trivial as the weather! Her observation is that the only two areas where this rule does not apply are where men discuss football in the pub and women remark about how ugly or fat they feel. Then disagreement is not only allowed, but positively encouraged! I wonder, though, if she were to rewrite the book today, whether she might also add a third category: 'online'?

So much of our online communication has become impersonal. It struggles to convey tone and can be read in the most cold and confrontational manner possible, instead of with the warmth with which it might have been intended. One of the most helpful pieces of advice I was given about such communication is that 'emails don't smile'. We could add, 'Neither do Tweets …'

This problem was exacerbated further during the Covid-19 outbreak. With much of the world's population locked down at home and not legally able to meet up with others, the majority of our communication was forced online. It was, therefore, perhaps not surprising that when we finally emerged from the first period of lockdown, the hostility in society had only increased. Some of the first public gatherings ended up with angry confrontations between protestors.

Dangerous untruths

However, while social media may be partly to blame for the increasing polarisation we see, I think there are deeper, more fundamental reasons. It would be too simplistic to blame it all on the internet. In *The Coddling of the American Mind*, Haidt and Lukianoff outline three particular untruths that have become increasingly popular as well as highlighting why they are so dangerous.

1. 'The untruth of fragility – what doesn't kill you makes you weaker'[71]

This deliberate inversion of a well-known saying implies that we are essentially fragile people who need to be protected from ideas that we find disagreeable. Yet shielding us from unpalatable ideas may actually be the reason *why* we have become so fragile. Haidt uses a helpful illustration to demonstrate how this works.

Increasing numbers of children have developed allergies to peanuts. One of the reasons for this seems to be that many parents, fearful that their child *may* have an allergy, protect their child from ever eating nuts. This lack of exposure in their formative years actually increases the chances that they will grow up to have a real allergy, for they haven't developed a protective immune response.[72]

In the same way, Haidt and Lukianoff say, we need exposure to ideas that we disagree with so that we learn how to handle such conflicts in an emotionally healthy way. Overly protecting people may actually cause more harm than good.

2. 'The untruth of emotional reasoning – always trust your feelings'[73]

We are encouraged to listen to our feelings and never question them. Yet Haidt shows how this idea cuts right against the basic principles of Cognitive Behavioural Therapy, where people are encouraged to challenge their feelings – especially when those feelings seem to be out of step with reality.

3. 'The untruth of us versus them – life is a battle between good people and evil people'[74]

In saying this, Haidt and Lukianoff don't deny the reality of good and evil as real categories that exist. What they critique is the simplistic division of the world into people who are either wholly good or wholly evil. I think it is this third untruth, in particular, that gets close to the heart of the problem in society today, and is so dangerous.

The problem with simplistic divisions

If we think that the world is divided simply into good people and evil people, then we tend to assume that we are in the first category, and that those we disagree with fall into the second: 'I'm good – you're evil.' Therefore, instead of thinking the best of our opponents, we tend to think the very worst. They aren't just wrong – they are a fascist, or a Marxist, or a transphobe, or a misogynist, or a racist, and so on.

The problem with such thinking is twofold. Firstly, we can often fail to see *any* possible good in others. Secondly, we can also fail to see any possible failings in *ourselves*.

Barak Obama, the former US President, put his finger on the issue when he said in a televised discussion:

This idea of your purity and you're never compromised and you're always politically woke, you should get over that quickly. The world is messy. There are ambiguities. People who do really good stuff have flaws. People who you are fighting may love their kids ... One danger among young people particularly on college campuses [is that they think] the way of me making change is to be as judgemental as possible about other people and that's enough. If I Tweet or hashtag about how you didn't do something right or use the wrong verb, I can sit back and feel pretty good about myself. 'Man, you see how woke I was, I called you out.' ... That's not activism. That's not bringing about change. If all you're doing is casting stones, you're probably not going to get that far. That's easy to do.[75]

The problem of this simplistic division of the world was revealed during the 2020 anti-racism protests in the UK. In the city of Bristol, a statue of a former slave trader had been very publicly and unceremoniously torn down by protestors and dumped into the harbour. In the following days, other statues came under threat as massive debates raged about whether they should also be removed or not.

In an effort to show that he was taking the protests seriously, the Mayor of London announced the setting up of a commission that would consider removing statues commemorating people who had associations with racism. However, it was pointed out that this could be problematic for the Mayor: according to this criterion, one of the statues that might have to be removed was one that he himself had unveiled less than two years previously.

Millicent Fawcett was a suffragette who fought for the right of women to vote. As such, she was rightly celebrated for standing against the oppression she experienced in her day. In fact, hers was the first statue of a woman to appear in London's Parliament Square. However, it was also revealed that she had held racist views and that her actions had directly led to the deaths of 25,000 black Africans in the Boer War in South Africa. So was Fawcett good or bad? Should she be celebrated or disparaged?

As discussion around other historical figures revealed, it is far too simplistic to divide the world in such a way.

Ultimately, many of our greatest heroes were also severely flawed. That is not to say that we should never remove a statue – I don't think that any of my Eastern European friends were upset at the removal of statues of Stalin after the fall of the Soviet Union. But it should cause us to stop and think about whether we may have divided the world too simplistically.

When we realise that other people are a more complex mix than we at first might have thought, this also causes us to consider that we ourselves might be. Someone who came to understand this deeply was the Russian author Alexander Solzhenitsyn.

I recently finished listening to an audio production of his greatest work, *The Gulag Archipelago*. It takes twenty-four hours to listen to even the abridged edition! In the work, he recounts his horrific experiences in the Gulag (the Soviet equivalent of the Nazi concentration camp). Part of my motivation to read it was that my own great-grandfather died in one.

Solzhenitsyn explains how the Soviet system was based on the simplistic division of society into the good and the bad. People were either part of the oppressors or part of the oppressed. Whole segments of society were arrested and forcibly shipped off to Siberia – my great-grandparents among them. Solzhenitsyn describes, in harrowing detail, his own journey there, and the sufferings and injustices that he experienced.

As a result, it would have been easy for Solzhenitsyn to simply rage against his oppressors and the political system that had created such evil. Incredibly, he doesn't, but rather explains:

> *So let the reader who expects this book to be a political exposé slam its covers shut right now.*
>
> *If only it were all so simple! If only there were evil people somewhere insidiously committing evil deeds, and it were necessary only to separate them from the rest of us and destroy them. But the line dividing good and evil cuts through the heart of every human being. And who is willing to destroy a piece of his own heart?*

That is not to say that all people are equally good or evil. Solzhenitsyn continues:

> *During the life of any heart this line keeps changing place; sometimes it is squeezed one way by exuberant evil and sometimes it shifts to allow enough space for good to flourish. One and the same human being is, at various ages, under various circumstances, a totally different human being. At times he is close to being a devil, at times to sainthood. But his name doesn't change, and to that name we ascribe the whole lot, good and evil.*
>
> *Socrates taught us: Know thyself!*

His conclusion is particularly sobering and especially relevant: 'Confronted by the pit into which we are about to toss those who have done us harm, we halt, stricken dumb: it is after all only because of the way things worked out that they were the executioners and we weren't.'[76]

Solzhenitsyn realised an uncomfortable truth: oppression and evil don't simply exist in the hearts of our enemies; they can exist in us too. Who is to say that in different circumstances we couldn't have been just like the people we are tempted to despise the most?

Is there any hope?

Is there any way out of this increasing polarisation in our society? Or will things just continue to get worse? Solzhenitsyn's book is a timely warning of where such ideas might take us.

However, Haidt and Lukianoff conclude their book by saying that we don't need to despair. Despite admitting that there are 'alarming trends … particularly … America's rising political polarization' and that 'these problems are serious, and we see no sign that [they] will be reversing in the next decade', they conclude, 'we are heartened by and persuaded by the cognitive psychologist Stephen Pinker's argument, in *Enlightenment Now*, that in the long run most things are getting better.'[77]

I find it rather interesting that their main reason for hoping that humanity will be ok is that a Canadian psychologist thinks the world is getting better! Though they do bring a thorough diagnosis of the problem, as is typical of Haidt, arguably this doesn't really offer any kind of solution at all. Indeed, there are some serious questions to ask of Pinker's ideas.

While it is true that Pinker makes a good case that many things have got better in our world,[78] this is obviously not the case in every area of life – just think of some of the environmental challenges that our world is facing. However, his attempt to show that this is all a result of the Enlightenment is most weak. Many of the roots of what he holds so highly, like liberal democracy, predate the Enlightenment, so couldn't have been caused by it. Neither is it correct to assume that the Enlightenment was mainly an atheistic project, as Pinker suggests. Many of its great thinkers, like Newton, Voltaire, Hume and Kant, certainly weren't atheists. In his brilliant review of Pinker's book, Nick Spencer of the Theos Thinktank explains, 'Under no stretching of the imagination could the Enlightenment be imagined to be an atheistic movement, for which Pinker is clearly straining to claim it.'[79]

In contrast to this, the secular historian Tom Holland has a different view of history. In his brilliant book *Dominion*,[80] he agrees that we can see many areas of progress in our world. However, unlike Pinker, he says that this hasn't happened because we got rid of Christianity, but because our world has been revolutionised by it. Indeed, the very idea of progress is profoundly Christian.

If he is right to think that the influence of Christianity in the past has caused the world to get better, what does it mean for society's rejection of Christianity today? Could this rejection be one of the reasons why some things seem to be getting worse? These are important questions to consider, as it is the very future of humanity that is at stake.

Jesus' verdict on humanity

To answer these questions, we need to look at what was so revolutionary about Christianity. Therefore, let's examine one particular revolutionary idea taught by Jesus and see its implications for our world.

Jesus is having a confrontation with a group of religious leaders. (It is interesting that the most hostile response to Jesus and his teaching came from those who were most religious in his society. If we find ourselves disillusioned by traditional religion, then we may find we have an unexpected affinity with Jesus.) The religious leaders are shocked that Jesus' followers disregard certain religious rituals: 'Why don't your disciples live according to the tradition of the elders instead of eating their food with defiled hands?' they ask, in a rather accusatory manner.

It should be noted that the issue here is not one of personal hygiene. Washing hands before eating is a very good idea, as we have become well aware. What Jesus challenges is the way in which these people use outward ceremonies to try to virtue-signal their own moral goodness, in an attempt to hide what they are really like. 'You have let go of the commands of God and are holding on to human traditions,' Jesus challenges them.

He then goes on to point out how these human traditions have led them to act in ways that are anything but good. In particular, he calls them out for how they have treated their own parents. Instead of using their money to care for their parents, as they have an obligation to do, they have devised a clever way of ring-fencing the money by devoting it to God. Of course, once their parents have died, they also have a way to 'un-devote it' and use it on themselves. Jesus shows them up for being the self-righteous hypocrites that they are. These religious leaders make a show of keeping ritually clean, so nothing bad will get into them, but Jesus reveals that the really bad stuff is already within them.

Jesus then turns to address the crowd of onlookers: 'Listen to me, everyone, and understand this. Nothing outside a person can defile them by going into them. Rather, it is what comes out of a person that defiles them.' Jesus' own followers are obviously confused by this because later on, in private, they ask him what he had meant. He responds by asking them, 'Don't you see that nothing that enters a person from the outside can defile them?' He continues, 'What comes out of a person is what defiles them. For it is from within, out of a person's heart, that evil thoughts come – sexual immorality, theft, murder, adultery, greed, malice, deceit, lewdness, envy, slander, arrogance and folly. All these evils come from inside and defile a person.'[81]

Jesus says that the problem of evil is not external, but internal. It is what goes on inside us that is the root of the problem. The evil in our world is not just in our structures and systems, or in other people whom we despise; it can also be in *us*.

The problem within

This uncomfortable realisation of our own capacity for evil is something that journalist Jon Ronson speaks of in his brilliant and insightful book *So You've Been Publicly Shamed*. In it, he looks at numerous incidents of people who have been shamed on social media and how that has had far-reaching and long-lasting implications for their lives. However, instead of pointing the finger at a small group of online trolls, he realises that we all have the capacity to destroy someone's life. He writes, 'The powerful, crazy, cruel people I usually write about tend to be in far-off places,' before coming to his uncomfortable conclusion: 'The powerful, crazy cruel people were now us.'[82]

Of course, we don't like hearing such things. Ronson explains, 'For years I've been writing stories about people abusing their power. When the people abusing their power were "over there", in the military or the pharmaceutical industry, everyone loved it … but as soon as I wrote that we were the ones abusing our power … people were saying that I must be a racist too.'[83]

Martin Lewis, of Money Saving Expert, revealed how hard it is to recognise our own failings through a fascinating Twitter poll: 'So far in this poll 95% of people believe they are a "decent and generally honest person" – yet only 16% of people in my earlier poll believe that over 90% of other people are. So, either we're over-inflating our own goodness, or under-appreciating it in others.'[84]

The difficulty admitting our own failings

Why do we often assume the best of ourselves and the worst of others? Why is it so hard to face up to our own failings? Why is it much easier to cast judgement on other people? To a degree this has always been the case, but I think it is a particular challenge in our present culture because there seems to be no way back from failure.

We do speak much about tolerance in contemporary society, but that tolerance only extends so far. Such tolerance is ultimately based on indifference, and it is hard to be indifferent about wrongdoing and injustice. So faced with things with which we profoundly disagree, the only option seems to be to call it out and ensure that the perpetrator is cancelled. There seems to be no opportunity for redemption or forgiveness.

Ian Dunt writes:

> *The social media frenzy around these stories [of public shaming] claims to be based on compassion. But it is in fact an extremely unforgiving culture. It defines people solely by the very worst thing they have ever said. It does not allow them to move on from it, ever.*
>
> *It doesn't matter how much you apologise. It doesn't matter how genuine your sorrow is. It doesn't matter how much you have listened or learned or improved yourself. Any evidence of impurity, no matter how dated, means you are cast out forever.*[85]

Douglas Murray agrees, pointing out why this problem may have arisen in a brilliant interlude in *The Madness of Crowds*:

> ... *we have created a world in which forgiveness has become almost impossible ... The Christian tradition ... stressed the desirability ... of forgiveness. Even to the point of infinite forgiveness. As one of the consequences of the death of God, Friedrich Nietzsche foresaw that people could find themselves stuck in cycles of Christian theology with no way out. Specifically that people would inherit the concepts of guilt, sin and shame but would be without the means of redemption which the Christian religion also offered. Today we do seem to live in a world where actions can have consequences that we could never have imagined, where guilt and shame are more at hand than ever, and where we have no means whatsoever of redemption. We do not know who could offer it.*[86]

Murray highlights that Christianity gives us not only the concepts of guilt and shame, but also the liberating offer of forgiveness. Without forgiveness, the best option is surely to hide our own failings, for fear of the shame and rejection that we would experience if they were revealed. We hope that by pointing out the failings of others, people will be distracted from seeing our own.

The freedom of forgiveness

To be able to face up to our own failures, we need to know that there is the possibility of forgiveness. Forgiveness does not mean we are indifferent to injustice – in fact, quite the opposite. Forgiveness is costly.

Christianity roots the possibility of our forgiveness in the death of Jesus. God can offer us forgiveness because he himself was publicly shamed *for* us. Ultimately, Jesus chose to die a horrific death in which he took upon himself our guilt and shame *so that* we might be forgiven. He took the ultimate consequences for what we have done *so that* we might not be condemned for them.

When we realise Jesus offers us the possibility of forgiveness and a fresh start, it makes it easier for us to face up to our own failings. We no longer have to virtue-signal our own goodness. We are accepted by God not because of what we have done, but because of what Jesus has done. In fact, the first step to becoming a Christian is to admit that we aren't the people we should be. We need to face up to our own failings and recognise our need for forgiveness.

This isn't easy. But it is, at least, *easier* to admit your failings to a God who loves you and is willing to forgive you, than it is to admit them to a Twitter mob that only wants to get you sacked.

God's forgiveness also means that it should be wonderful to be part of a Christian church. It should be a community of people who have come to understand that they are flawed, but also forgiven. This leaves no space for self-righteousness, virtue-signalling or judgementalism, all of which are incompatible with following Jesus. While this may not be how we perceive the church to be, sometimes our perceptions can be wrong.

I remember meeting Jane at the end of a talk I had given at Leeds University's Christian Union and hearing her story. When she came to university, she was fearful of Christians, believing them all to be homophobic. In fact, she was going to ask to be placed in a hall of residence where there weren't any because she felt she needed a safe space away from their bigotry. However, she never got around to it and on the first day at uni discovered, to her horror, that she was living right next door to a very active member of the Christian Union!

However, over the coming weeks, her preconceptions were dismantled by the love and care her neighbour showed to her. Despite the fact that they had very different ideas on many issues, not least on the Bible's teaching on sexuality, they formed an unlikely friendship. As a result, she had started going to the Christian Union, though she was still very sceptical of much of what she was hearing.

She commented that some members of the LGBT society (of which she was also a part) had reacted very negatively and even dissociated themselves from her on discovering this. Yet she concluded, 'I still come, though, because I have found, to my surprise, that this is the most welcoming and inclusive group on campus.'

What made that group so welcoming? They were simply a group of people who were willing to acknowledge their own failings because they had experienced the real forgiveness and love of Jesus.

It is both this realisation of our own guilt and the discovery of such forgiveness that has the power to heal our societies – and, indeed, the world. God's forgiveness not only allows us to face up to our own failings (instead of distracting others from them by pointing the finger) but enables us to love and forgive others as well.

Embracing the forgiveness of Jesus doesn't mean that we no longer care about issues of inequality and injustice in society. Forgiveness is not the same as tolerance. We should be passionate about seeking to make our society a safer, fairer place. However, we do that best from a position of humility that accepts that we ourselves may be part of the problem. We also need to be ready to offer forgiveness to those to whom we might naturally be opposed. Such an attitude has the possibility to bring about lasting change and real reconciliation.

5

Making sense of suffering

Is there any purpose in our pain?

There are some phone conversations you will never forget.

I had been spending an enjoyable afternoon at home, watching the rugby, when I noticed a missed call from a friend. I thought for a moment that she must have been ringing to discuss the game. She was also an avid rugby fan and, being Welsh, we often enjoyed some good banter – especially when Wales were playing England. However, as soon as I called back, I could tell from her voice that she wasn't wanting to talk about the rugby, but something far more serious.

Over the last year, her daughter had been battling a rare form of cancer. They had not long returned from the United States, where she had received specialist treatment and, just two weeks previously, had been given the all clear. Yet now they had been called back into the hospital.

The cancer hadn't gone; it had spread. It was terminal. Ceri was going to die.

I struggled to know what to say, as I tried to comprehend their emotional turmoil and began to think of the painful journey that lay ahead of them.

Asking questions

Whoever we are, wherever we live and whatever we believe, we cannot avoid suffering. The question is not if, but when and how, we will face it. When we do suffer, one of the first questions we ask is *why*? Why them? Why me? Why this? Why now? Is there a way that we can make sense of what is happening to us? Is there some purpose behind it, or is it ultimately meaningless?

According to many atheistic thinkers, suffering and pain is ultimately futile. They say we shouldn't seek to find purpose or meaning in it because life is ultimately meaningless. David Benatar, the South African philosopher, puts it starkly in his book *The Human Predicament*: 'Life is meaningless.' He goes on to speak of the 'cosmic insignificance and the pointlessness of the entire human endeavour'.[87]

The American physicist Lawrence Krauss agrees: 'We are a 1% bit of pollution within the universe. We are completely insignificant.'[88]

'What is the meaning of the universe and of life?' asks Alex Rosenberg, in his book *An Atheist's Guide to Reality*. 'There is none,' he responds. 'Why am I here? Just dumb luck,' he concludes.[89]

While all three thinkers are to be admired for their consistency, are we content to think that our painful experiences of life – indeed, our entire lives – are really pointless? Does nothing ultimately matter? Is there really no hope? Atheism holds little comfort when faced with the reality of pain. Maybe this is why, in the face of real suffering, people often turn to religion rather than away from it. Atheism can seem like an attractive position to hold in the comfort of a lecture room, but less so in the painful realities of life. We want to try to make sense of what is going on. We want answers. We want there to be some purpose to our pain. If atheism doesn't work for the painful realities of life, then why should we bother with it in the real world of pain and injustice?

Looking for answers

Each of the world's major religions seeks to make sense of pain and suffering. Indeed, Buddhism was, from its inception, a direct response to it. According to Buddhist tradition, it was after being confronted by the reality of suffering (in particular, old age, sickness and death), that the Buddha left the palace where he had grown up in comfort and became a wandering ascetic and teacher. He taught that suffering was caused by desire and that the way to respond to it was to eliminate all desire.

Along with other Eastern religions, Buddhism also taught the idea of reincarnation based on karma. According to this concept, suffering is a punishment for things we have done, either in this or a previous life. This idea can be very attractive, and not just to those from an Eastern cultural background.

I was once chatting to a fellow passenger at London Gatwick airport over breakfast. He revealed how he was drawn to the idea of karma as it helped him to feel that there was some purpose and meaning to the world's suffering, and that it was a way of justice being done.

Islam's response to suffering is to say that everything that happens is the will of Allah. Therefore, when we suffer, we shouldn't ask questions, but rather submit ourselves to whatever Allah has willed to happen. Indeed, the very word 'Islam' means 'to submit' and one of the phrases most often spoken by a Muslim is *Insha'Allah*, meaning 'If God wills'.

This was precisely the response of one grieving parent when interviewed on the TV news shortly after their son had been killed in the horrific Malaysia Airlines disaster in Ukraine. It may provide comfort to know that God has a purpose behind what has happened, even if we can't understand what it is.

Some Christian responses to suffering can sound similar to this Islamic one. They too can speak of everything that happens as being the 'will of God' and can be quick to quote the Bible's teaching that 'in all things God works for the good',[90] implying that everything happens for some good reason.

Questioning the answers

On one level, I can see a certain attraction to all these responses to suffering. Each of them seeks to give some sense of purpose to our pain and to help us to feel that what we might be going through isn't futile or pointless. However, on another level, do they really help, especially when we are confronted with the reality of deep suffering in our own personal lives?

Buddhism may teach us to deny our desire and see suffering as an illusion, but does that mean that our feelings of anguish, pain and frustration are actually inappropriate responses? Do they show that we are just not enlightened?

The concept of karma may teach us that suffering is deserved, and that may help explain suffering that happens to others, especially those we don't know and won't meet. However, what about when it happens to us, or those close to us? Could such a view actually diminish our compassion for those who are suffering?

A friend of mine, who has spent much of his life working in East Asia, recounted how a minibus full of his colleagues and their children had been involved in a very tragic accident there. A number were killed immediately, and others were left badly injured. However, despite the seriousness of the situation, many of the bystanders refused to go to their aid, for fear of interfering with their karma. They believed the victims were getting what they deserved. I am certainly not saying that everyone in that region would respond in such a way. Many people can show compassion in spite of their beliefs. But is it too much to hope that one's compassion – the very best of human behaviour – might actually arise from what we believe about reality?

Similarly, Islam's standpoint of everything happening due to the will of Allah can lead to a fatalistic view of suffering. In turn, this could possibly lead to a failure to take practical steps that would actually help prevent or alleviate suffering.

A good illustration of this is my taxi driver's response, on a recent trip to the Middle East. He looked rather offended when I put my seatbelt on as I got into the car, because he took this as a sign that I was doubting his driving ability. (To be honest, a few minutes and one very near miss later, I *was* questioning his driving ability!) I asked why he didn't think we needed to wear a seatbelt. He told me that the timing of when we die is down to the will of Allah, and therefore a seatbelt wouldn't make any difference.

In the same way, a Christian response that emphasises the will of God in all things can feel inadequate, and even insensitive, when it comes to real experiences of pain.

One summer, I was enjoying a week away in the mountains of the north of England when I received a text from a good friend. They had just come home to discover, to their horror, that their teenage son had taken his own life. I was totally stunned at the news. The next morning, I drove straight down to be with them. I will never forget what it was like to sit with them in their pain and agony. There had been absolutely no previous indication that this might happen. The shock was immense. The pain was raw. Our words were few.

Was this the will of God? Was it all going to work together for good? Did God have some purpose in causing this to happen? All of these questions seemed shallow and unsayable in the face of such anguish. None of these questions were going to bring their son back. None of them seemed at all helpful in the moment. Instead, we simply sat, mostly in silence, as we came to terms with the horror of what had happened.

I have often reflected on that moment. If our beliefs about pain and suffering are unsayable in the face of real pain, then maybe we need to think again.

Suffering and the Christian faith

Let's revisit the Christian understanding of suffering to see if it could give us more than superficial platitudes, actually helping to equip us when we go through suffering times ourselves.

One of the most helpful passages in the Bible about this subject is the one from which I quoted earlier about things working together for good. Although this verse hasn't always been used in a helpful way, when understood in its wider context, it is actually incredibly helpful. It is part of a letter written by the Apostle Paul to a group of Christians living in Rome in the first century. He begins by stating, 'I consider that our present sufferings are not worth comparing with the glory that will be revealed in us.'[91]

It might be easy to dismiss these words if we didn't first know something about who wrote them. It is easy to talk glibly about suffering when we are not actually going through any.

A few weeks ago, I was on holiday and enjoying a sunny day on the beach when my wife suggested that I use that time to get some inspiration for the next chapter of my book. I explained that I had already finished the chapter on *happiness* and I wasn't sure what inspiration the beach would give for the next chapter on *suffering*!

Paul, the author of the above passage, was not inspired to write his words from a deckchair on a Mediterranean beach, distant from and immune to the painful realities of life. Indeed, ever since Paul's well-documented and dramatic conversion to Christianity, his life had been characterised by pain. Some of this suffering had been inflicted by others – including physical attacks, beatings and unjust imprisonments. However, for other elements of his suffering, there didn't appear to be anyone to blame – he had a life-long struggle with an incurable and debilitating physical condition, and a shipwreck during a storm nearly claimed his life. Paul wrote from deep personal experience. Yet his beliefs weren't destroyed by his sufferings. Rather, they helped him make sense of them.

I am actually writing these words not from the beach, but on a dark and wet winter's day. Britain is in a strict lockdown as the death rate from Covid-19 has reached a record high. A friend needs an operation, but can't because the hospitals are overrun. Just yesterday, I heard the shocking news of a family friend's sudden death from a heart attack. My wife might lose her job so, as we look ahead, life seems very uncertain. How can Paul's words help us make sense of all this?

Our suffering is bad

Paul continues, 'For the creation was subjected to frustration…'[92] Some versions of the Bible use the word 'futility'. This may seem close to the atheistic view that life is ultimately futile. However, there is a key difference. Whereas the atheistic belief is that life has *always* been futile, the Bible says it has not always been this way. The implication is that this world as we know it is *not* what it was meant to be.

According to Genesis, the first book of the Bible, God created a world that is good – a world free from the frustrations and futility that we now experience. Into that world God created people – to enjoy it, to enjoy him and to enjoy each other. He also gave humans a choice: to live in that world *his* way, or to live in it *their own* way.

This choice seems a risky move on God's part. Why give people choice if he knew they could use it to screw things up so spectacularly? However, choice and love go together; you can't have one without the other. By giving people the freedom to truly love him and each other, God also gave them the freedom not to do so. The tragedy of human history is that we have so often chosen the latter.

The consequences of that have been catastrophic – not only for us and our relationships, but also for the whole of creation. Nothing is the way it should be, and these consequences are real. Like a virus that ends up infecting every operational aspect of a computer, so humanity's rejection of God has affected every aspect of our world.

While it may be easy to quickly dismiss the Bible's account of the origins of our world as implausible and then depressing, I find that actually it clearly makes sense of my experiences of life. When we stood by the grave of my friend's son, I instinctively felt that this *wasn't* the way things should be. If the Bible's account of our world is true, then we are right in feeling that. This *isn't* the way God wants the world to be. Something has gone wrong. So much of what happens in our world is frustrating, futile and unjust. This should make us angry.

I find the Bible's view of the world far more real and comforting in the face of suffering than any other perspective. It gives me an explanation for the way I feel when I suffer difficulty, and confirms that my default reaction to suffering is, in fact, right.

Suffering will not be here for ever

Paul further states, 'We know that the whole creation has been groaning as in the pains of childbirth right up to the present time.'[93] While Paul speaks of the whole of creation 'groaning' in frustration, he adds the words 'as in the pains of childbirth'. This tells us something significant about the Christian concept of suffering. In a hospital, the suffering experienced on the maternity ward is very different to that experienced elsewhere around the building. It is not because it is necessarily less painful (just ask any mother!), but because the pain of childbirth is directly linked to the imminent hope of new life.

Paul writes of the 'hope that the creation itself will be liberated from its bondage to decay and brought into the freedom and glory of the children of God', and that 'we wait eagerly for our adoption to sonship, the redemption of our bodies.'[94] The world we live in is not the way it once was, but nor is it the way it will one day be.

As I continue to write this chapter, I have just received news that a man known to some friends has been tragically killed while cycling home from work in Wales. In the BBC article about the incident, his family spoke of their devastation, but also added that they 'do not grieve without hope'.[95] Christianity doesn't deny the pain of suffering and loss, but it does offer hope in the midst of it.

This hope, as we shall see in chapter ten, is not for some spiritual dimension that continues beyond death. Rather, it is for the renewal and transformation of this damaged and hurting world. It is a physical hope for this broken world and for our broken bodies. Frustration and futility will not have the final say. Thankfully, they are not the end of the story!

Indeed, Paul writes that our experiences of suffering are 'not worth comparing' with what God has in store for us one day! His intention is, for sure, not to minimise the experiences that we go through in the present – he knew first-hand how painful they could be. Rather, he wants to maximise the hope that we can have if we know Jesus.

I have never liked the winter. Long, warm and sunny days must be preferable to cold, dark, winter ones. As a child, I dreamed that, one day, I could move location every six months between the southern and northern hemispheres to live in a perpetual summer. While that could be possible (and I have certainly enjoyed some mid-winter breaks in warmer places), I have realised that one of the advantages of going through the experience of winter is that it makes my appreciation of summer even greater. In fact, on a cold, grey, winter's day like today, the hope of spring to come makes life seem more bearable. It fills me with a sense of hope and joy, despite the dismal rain outside.

The Bible story says that we can look forward to an eternal spring to come. The knowledge of that real hope can give us joy even in, or rather *especially in*, the midst of suffering here and now.

When Ceri received the devastating news that her cancer was terminal, she wrote these words on her social media accounts: 'This isn't the news I thought I would be sharing three weeks from finding out my scans were clear, but the reality of life means that unfortunately it is.' After explaining how the cancer had spread and how she had months to live, she concluded with these words: 'My wise Daddy said this to me moments after we got this news … It was never meant to be about this life anyway. This is just a blip on the road to eternity and we're all just passing through. I'm confident that heaven will be infinitely better and am excited to see Jesus face to face.'

How we respond to suffering matters

As I said earlier, many people quote 'In all things God works for the good' in such a way that makes Paul seem rather glib. They do so as if whatever happens to us in life, we just need to say, 'It's all good'!

An old version of the Bible translates the verse this way: 'And we know that all things work together for good to those who love God.'[96] The problem with this translation is that it sounds a bit like the concept of karma that we thought about earlier – that if you love God, then things will work for your good. But what about when things don't seem to be working for our good? Do we simply conclude that we can't be loving God enough?

The rest of the Bible gives us *no* assurance that loving God means that only good things will happen to us. Indeed, one Bible writer puzzles over the fact that so often bad things seem to happen to good people while good things happen to bad people.[97] Far from guaranteeing our enjoyment of good things, loving and following God will often mean the opposite. Most of the first generation of Christians (and many since, including present-day Christians) have suffered and been persecuted precisely because of their faith.

A more modern Bible version translates the verse as: 'And we know that in all things God works for the good of those who love him.'[98] Here, it is not the 'things' that are working for our good, in some impersonal and abstract way, but God himself. However, that still leaves us with a problem: when we think the happenings in our lives don't seem good, how is God working in them for our good?

One way to resolve this is to think of our perspective on suffering. Is what *seems* bad to us, from our perspective, actually *good* when seen from God's? There are times when, with the benefit of hindsight, this is the case. Looking back at things that seemed bad to me at the time, I can see they ultimately worked for my good. For instance, a few years ago, I was distraught when a job opportunity fell through and a relationship came to an end. Yet now, I can look back and be thankful to God that they did for everyone concerned.

Difficulty comes, though, when we try to extrapolate this thinking to every experience of suffering. Should I tell my friends who so tragically lost their son that this was really God working for their good – if only they could see it from his perspective? Or what about those who are the victims of horrific physical and sexual abuse. Should we tell them that this really was for their good – and they will come to see that … eventually? Both would seem abhorrent expressions in response to suffering of this magnitude.

However, there is another way of translating this verse – one that not only translates well the original language that the Bible was written in, but also fits more consistently with what the rest of the Bible teaches.[99] It is: 'in all things God works together with those who love him to bring about what is good'.[100]

Understood this way, this verse is not saying that all things that happen are good if only we could see them in a certain way or from God's perspective. Indeed, many things that happen are horrific, painful, frustrating and futile. The Bible tells us there are many things in this world that grieve and anger God. Therefore, we are not to sit passively by while God 'does his thing', hoping that one day he might be able to turn around the situation. Rather, God calls us to work *in partnership* with him, responding to suffering and pain in a way that can, ultimately, bring good to others and to the world. We cannot change what might have happened to us, but we can, with God's help and power, bring about real change in this broken world.

As a promising young gymnast, Rachael Denhollander was abused by the USA gymnastics team doctor, Larry Nassar. Yet her courage encouraged hundreds of other women to come forward to testify against him, eventually leading to his life imprisonment. Rachael now works to bring about justice for abuse victims and to help organisations address leadership failures which facilitate such abuse. Her belief in the ultimate justice of God motivates her to work for justice here and now. Her conviction in the infinite value of every human being is a driving force behind her desire to protect and speak up for the most vulnerable. In response to the horrific suffering that Rachael experienced, she is working in partnership with God to bring about good.

This is also the case for my friends whom I mentioned earlier in this chapter. While they will never 'get over' the pain of losing their son, they have continued to pour out their lives, with compassion and empathy, in serving and helping other young people. They cannot bring back their son, but their work has helped hundreds of others, some of whom might otherwise have ended up in similar situations of suicidal desperation.

Despite being given just a few months to live, Ceri went on to live for another year. In that time, she invested in her friends and family. She lived long enough to witness the birth of her niece and the marriage of her best friend. She frequently shared, through social media posts, the journey that she was on. Although the photos revealed her physical deterioration, they also often showed a beaming smile. At the end of each post, she wrote, '#choosejoy'. Her hope and joy in the face of her suffering touched and impacted the lives of many others. Indeed, others came to find hope themselves through the hope they witnessed in Ceri.

Our suffering should remind us of Jesus

It is all too easy to forget that the very symbol of Christianity is one of horrific suffering. Roman crucifixion is one of the most painful forms of execution ever invented. Why on earth would anyone want to make an instrument of torture the symbol of their faith?

That was certainly the thinking of one Muslim friend who told me, 'I could never believe that Jesus is God.'

'Why not?' I asked.

'I could never believe in a God who could be weak or suffer. Allah cannot suffer. I find the idea of your God dying on the cross offensive,' he explained.

As I reflected on what he said, I realised that actually Jesus dying on the cross *helps* me to believe in God. The God revealed in the Bible is not immune to suffering. He doesn't sit above it in holy isolation from our pain. The heart of the Christian message is a God who has experienced the full range of human suffering.

Shortly after Jesus' birth, he narrowly avoided being caught up in a genocide. He lived his first few years as a refugee. The rest of his life was spent in a country occupied by a cruel foreign power. He experienced rejection, misunderstanding, betrayal, injustice and torture. Ultimately, he experienced crucifixion – a form of execution so *excruciating* that we derive that very word from it.

The shocking message of the Bible is that God himself has suffered with us. We don't stand alone in our pain. He knows what it is like; he can understand completely. This knowledge can totally change our perspective on the matter.

Edward Shillito was a poet who lived and fought in the First World War. As he reflected on the horrors that he had experienced, and questioned how he could go on believing in God, he wrote these words:

The other gods were strong; but Thou wast weak;
They rode, but Thou didst stumble to a throne;
But to our wounds only God's wounds can speak,
And not a god has wounds, but Thou alone.[101]

Yet it is not simply that, in Jesus, God suffered *with* us. The Bible says that he also suffered *for* us.

As we have seen, our world is broken because we have chosen to become disconnected from the God who made us. In our most honest moments, we have to admit that sometimes we are part of the problem. Our words and actions can sometimes cause hurt and pain to others. At other times, it's not so much what we do, but what we *fail* to do that causes or exacerbates other people's pain. Such guilt should rightly cut us off from God for ever.

Yet, despite everything, God wanted us to be reconnected to him. On the cross, Jesus took the ultimate consequences for what we have done. The suffering that should rightly be ours, if justice were to be done, was willingly experienced by him, so that we might be spared it.

Once we have come to recognise this, and to experience God's wonderful forgiveness, then we can look forward to the future with hope. Jesus' suffering means that suffering will be no more one day! Jesus' death means that death itself has been defeated. That Jesus also came alive again from the dead means we can know that there is life to come. No matter what we go through, the certainty of that hope, and the knowledge that God understands what we are going through, can make all the difference.

God's desire is to work in partnership with us to bring about good in this world and in the lives of others: 'In all things God works together with those who love him to bring about what is good.'[102]

6

Making sense of myself

How do I discover my true identity?

I arrived home from an international trip to discover an unexpectedly large pile of post in my letterbox. As I started to open each letter, I was at first confused and then increasingly concerned. Though all of the letters were addressed to me, the contents referred to numerous bank accounts, credit cards and mobile phone contracts – none of which I had any previous knowledge of! I soon realised the problem. Someone had stolen my identity.

As I phoned the relevant companies to report what had happened, a slightly surreal conversation unfolded with one particular bank's call assistant:

Me: I'm ringing to report that someone has
           stolen my identity and fraudulently
           opened a bank account in my name.

Assistant: I'm very sorry to hear that, Sir.
             Firstly, I just need to ask you a few
             questions for security. What is your
             memorable word?

             I tell them my memorable word.

Assistant: I'm sorry, that doesn't match the word
             on the account.

Me: That's because I am not the person
             who set up the account!

Assistant: Who are you then?

Me: [getting rather exasperated]
             I'm Michael Ots!

Assistant: Ok, no worries at all. Let's see ... can
             you tell me the name of your first pet?

After some time, the assistant finally became convinced that I was the *real* Michael Ots, and thankfully all was resolved at no cost to me. But the incident did get me thinking about the whole question of identity. What is my identity? What really makes me 'me'? What makes me different to you, or to anyone else?

Much of my life is spent working with students. The university years can be a time when people ask this question with real urgency. Away from home, often for the first time, students have the opportunity to discover who they really are – but who really knows them? Their family knew who they used to be, but maybe they now want an opportunity to become someone else. Their friends and course mates may know a different version of them – the one they are trying hard to present – but can anyone really claim to know someone they've only known for a few weeks or months? When we stop to think about it, do we even know ourselves?

However, we discover that these questions are not confined to the university campus. We might assume that once we graduate, we will have all our questions figured out, but many of life's turning points can prompt us to ask fresh questions of our identity. Whether it's changing careers, losing a job, living with a chronic illness, getting married, having children, saying goodbye to our children, or finding ourselves unexpectedly alone, external circumstances can force us to revaluate our own sense of identity. Some might feel within themselves a profound sense of dissatisfaction or disconnection.

So how do we find our true identity? How do we discover who we really are? The way people have sought to answer these questions differs from generation to generation and from culture to culture.

Look out

One way to discover our identity is effectively to 'look out' to others. We need to listen to who others tell us we are. Our identity is something that is given to us by those around us – by our parents or carers, and through the expectations of our culture.

While this is particularly the case in non-Western cultures today, we still see traces of this way of thinking in Western culture by considering people's surnames. Many family names in Britain and subsequently America were originally descriptive of the occupation of your family. The Bakers baked, the Cooks cooked, the Smiths were blacksmiths and so on. From birth, your very name told you what your future profession would likely be. Your identity was given to you. (I am not sure how accurate this use of descriptive family names is in other cultures. I made a discovery that the German surname *Schweinsteiger* can be literally translated 'pig climber'! That would be a strange way to 'earn your bacon' …)

This expectation that we will continue in the family trade can still exist today. As a teenager, I was told that I would probably become a teacher, for that was the profession of both my parents. I remember determining that I would, as a result, never go into teaching. It only occurred to me recently that, although I don't work in a school, I am effectively … a teacher!

There are certain strengths to such an ordering of society. Valuable skills get passed down through succeeding generations. Life is, in some ways, simpler in that people do not have to discover their identity, but simply live within the identity they have been given.

However, there are issues of choice with our identity being formed in this way. In such a culture, choosing our identity would be as strange an idea as choosing a brand of toothpaste in North Korea – there is no choice; all get the same. What if we don't want to be who our families or society expect us to be?

At college, one of my course mates revealed that he didn't actually want to study the course he was on. His parents had told him that he must for he was to continue in his father's line of work. Sadly, the pressure of parental expectation actually contributed to him having a mental breakdown.

This cultural expectation forms the background to the beautiful biographical drama *October Sky*. It is based on the true story of Homer Hickam, a coal miner's son living in 1950s West Virginia. Inspired by the launch of Sputnik 1, Homer becomes fascinated by rocketry. However, the expectations of his culture, and in particular his father, are for him to work as a coal miner like everyone else in his town. It takes considerable courage, and the encouragement of his visionary schoolteacher, to overcome these cultural pressures and eventually go on to become an engineer at NASA.

How culture defines us can extend well beyond our profession. It can also involve expectations about many other life choices, including our sexual identity, marriage choices and decisions about having children. It can even go right down to the more minor details, like the clothes that we wear. Many of us would find it restrictive to have our identity defined by our culture. Understandably, we might hope that there is another way of discovering who we are.

Look in

If the drawbacks with such a way of defining one's identity seem clear to us, that is probably because, like many in the West, we have adopted a very different approach. In fact, it is almost completely the opposite. Instead of *looking out* to find our identity in who others tell us we are, we now assume that we find our identity by *looking in* and discovering who we ourselves want to be.

Such an approach is not only now permissible, but actually celebrated. As in *October Sky*, many great movies and books are based on this idea. Another such story is that of *Billy Elliot*. In it, a boy from a working-class town in the north of England defies the demands of his father, and the expectations of his culture, by becoming a ballet dancer. As we watch, we can long for such characters to be able to break free from societal expectations and become who they want to be. Through such films, and other influences, we too are encouraged to believe that we can be whoever we want to be, and that no one can tell us otherwise.

It is worth noting that there is much about this that is liberating. I am glad that we live in a culture where we have real freedom to be ourselves, rather than simply having to live up to society's expectations of who we are or what we should do. My wife would be a good current example of this. As a female airline pilot, 95% of her colleagues are men. In fact, despite her uniform, she has often been mistaken by passengers as one of the cabin crew.[103]

Yet while it is good that we live in a society that affords us a degree of freedom to determine who we want to be, it is worth asking some questions about how far this freedom can realistically go.

Can I really be anything I want?

While it is popular to believe that we can be *whoever* we want to be, is this really true? Growing up, I discovered that I had flat feet. While not a great problem in comparison to what others face, it did mean that I normally came last in races on school sports day, and I often got laughed at for the way my legs splayed out sideways as I ran. As much as I might have wanted it, I knew that 'Olympic sprinter' was not going to be part of my identity. Thankfully, while my feet are still flat, my legs are above average in strength and my lung capacity is unusually high. So while I have never been a runner, I have for many years been a keen long-distance cyclist. Indeed, my love of cycling has become an important part of my identity.

Surely there are some identities, by dint of our age, experience or physique, that we could never carry off, no matter how much we wanted them or how hard we tried? In fact, suggesting someone can be whoever they want could actually be harmful, in that it builds unrealistic expectations that ultimately end in disappointment. It also ignores the reality that at least *part* of who we are is shaped by who we *physically* are. The real 'me' is not some abstract concept, rather my physical body partly determines who I am. Perhaps rather than asking, 'Who do I want to be?', and trying to conform our bodies to a particular identity we might desire, it is better to simply ask, 'Who am I already?'

Contrary to what some might say, we can't just decide to be whoever we want. Certain aspects of our identity are given to us through no choice of our own – our biological sex, physical make-up, mental capacity, natural temperament and certain natural abilities. We may not be happy with all of these attributes and may wish that they were different; they are, nonetheless, still an essential part of who we are.

Is it wise to not listen to those around me?

We have seen that others may pressurise us to be who *they* want us to be, but there is another danger: that we ignore the well-intentioned advice of those who know us well.

Imagine I fancy myself as a comedian and start telling jokes. The trouble is that no one ever laughs at my jokes but groans and rolls their eyes. What do I do? I could choose to ignore them because 'I can be whoever I want to be', so keep telling them my jokes anyway. But if I do that, I'll soon be telling jokes to myself; I won't have an audience at all.

Sometimes, we *need* others to help us discover who we are. Indeed, ignoring completely what other people say may not be our hoped pathway to freedom, but rather a quick route to disaster.

Can I really be free from society's expectations?

It is easy to look back on previous cultures, see how society pressurised people to conform to certain expectations and assume that such a thing doesn't happen today. Yet are we free from societal expectations, or have those expectations just changed? While we may *think* that we are free to be ourselves, are we sometimes just being conformed to a different set of societal expectations?

For instance, in a previous generation, there would have been a pressure on women to give up work to bring up children. Now, in some contexts, they can be pressurised to forgo having children at all to further their career plans. Or, in some cultures, it would be incredibly difficult, and even dangerous, for someone to come out as gay. In the West, that is now not typically the case. However, a friend of mine commented that he has sometimes found hostility not to his being gay, but to his decision (based on his religious convictions) to remain celibate.

Look up

When seeking to discover our identity, we can see the problems with only *looking out* and listening to what others say, or to *looking in* and listening to how we ourselves feel. What if real identity could be found by *looking up* and listening to what God says, and by grounding our identity there?

Let's examine one particular encounter from Jesus' life to see what this looks like in practice.

Jesus entered Jericho and was passing through. A man was there by the name of Zacchaeus; he was a chief tax collector and was wealthy. He wanted to see who Jesus was, but because he was short he could not see over the crowd. So he ran ahead and climbed a sycamore-fig tree to see him, since Jesus was coming that way.

When Jesus reached the spot, he looked up and said to him, 'Zacchaeus, come down immediately. I must stay at your house today.' So he came down at once and welcomed him gladly.

All the people saw this and began to mutter, 'He has gone to be the guest of a sinner.'

But Zacchaeus stood up and said to the Lord, 'Look, Lord! Here and now I give half of my possessions to the poor, and if I have cheated anybody out of anything, I will pay back four times the amount.'

Jesus said to him, 'Today salvation has come to this house, because this man, too, is a son of Abraham. For the Son of Man came to seek and to save the lost.'[104]

In this encounter, we see how Jesus can, at one and the same time, affirm, challenge and transform our identity, and so help us to embrace our true identity.

Affirming our identity

When we read through the accounts of Jesus' life, it is fascinating to see the various ways that people try to get in contact with him. As we looked at in a previous chapter, some people had to destroy the roof of a house to get their paralysed friend to Jesus. In this story, Zacchaeus has to resort to climbing a tree to get a glimpse of him.[105]

Why did Zacchaeus have to climb the tree? Why couldn't he have pushed his way to the front? I wonder whether this was because at least some people in the crowd deliberately wanted to stop him from getting near to Jesus. We can see from their later response that they despised Zacchaeus as a 'sinner'. This dislike was not without reason – Zacchaeus was a tax collector. Holding this profession in first-century Palestine would have had a huge impact on the way people viewed you. A tax collector was a man who had not only colluded with the occupying Roman forces but had also become rich by extorting his own people. Rather than the general dislike that you might have for a traffic warden, this was more like the contempt we might feel for a loan shark.

Jesus' actions are therefore all the more remarkable. Stopping beneath the tree, he looks straight at Zacchaeus and invites himself round for dinner. To a Brit, this could seem rather rude. You don't go inviting yourself round to people's houses; you wait for them to invite you! However, Jesus' request was not rude, but rather incredibly kind because being a guest of someone in that culture was a way of showing them real dignity and respect. This can still be true in other cultures today, as I have discovered on my own travels.[106] Jesus' decision to invite himself to Zacchaeus' house was a significant way of affirming him. As we see so many times in the gospel accounts, Jesus has time for someone who would otherwise have been excluded.

Sometimes, the attitudes and actions of others can leave us feeling like Zacchaeus. Maybe you have been openly rejected, or more subtly 'given the cold shoulder'. This may at times be unfair, but sometimes it may be with good reason. Perhaps things in your life have led others to come to their conclusion about you. Yet even if their attitude towards you is at least partially warranted, as it was in Zacchaeus' case, experiencing the rejection of others is still incredibly painful.

How amazing, therefore, that Jesus doesn't view us as others do. He treats us with dignity and respect. As we saw in chapter one, that's because, whoever we are, we were created in the image of God and therefore have infinite value. If your sense of identity and value has been damaged in any way by the negative actions of others, whether family, friends or colleagues, realise that there is one who doesn't see you in that way. God sees what others may have lost sight of: that you have special and significant meaning to him.

Challenging our identity

Jesus' attitude towards Zacchaeus is so different to that of the crowd. Their assessment of Zacchaeus is that he is a 'sinner', but Jesus says that he is 'lost'. They are motivated by condemnation; Jesus is motivated by compassion. This does not mean that Zacchaeus isn't a sinner – in fact, the rest of the Bible reveals that sin is a condition universal to humanity. However, a condemning or judgemental approach from another is rarely successful in enabling us to address our wrong.

Out of compassion, Jesus neither condemns nor condones Zacchaeus, but helps him to confront the fact that all is not right in his life. Zacchaeus' problem was not simply that he had extorted others – that was merely a symptom of a deeper disease. His main problem was that he had built his identity on the wrong foundation.

The first thing we learn about Zacchaeus' identity is that he is wealthy. It seems that Zacchaeus had made acquiring material wealth central to who he was. Yet in an effort to gain that wealth, he had sacrificed so much along the way. Not only had he sided with the Romans against his own people, but he had cheated his fellow citizens. Consequently, this left him despised and alone.

David Foster Wallace, an American author and professor, seems to have recognised how destructive it is to build your identity on the wrong thing. During his commencement speech at Kenyon College, Ohio, he said:

> *In the day-to-day trenches of adult life, there is actually no such thing as atheism ... Everybody worships. The only choice we get is what to worship.*
>
> *And the compelling reason for maybe choosing some sort of god ... is that pretty much anything else you worship will eat you alive.*
>
> *If you worship money and things, if they are where you tap real meaning in life, then you will never have enough ...*

Worship your body and beauty and sexual allure and you will always feel ugly. And when time and age start showing, you will die a million deaths before they finally kill you ...

Worship power, you will end up feeling weak and afraid, and you will need ever more power over others to numb you to your own fear.

Worship your intellect, being seen as smart, you will end up feeling stupid, a fraud, always on the verge of being found out.[107]

Whatever we make the foundation of our identity will become the functional god in our lives. Yet far from giving us a solid and stable foundation, we find that, ultimately, it will crumble. There is nothing wrong with money, sex, power or intelligence in and of themselves. But to make any of these things the centre of identity is dangerous. Not only will they never really satisfy us, but we will often sacrifice so much in our efforts to try to get and then to keep them.

One of my favourite films of all time is *Cool Runnings* – the hilarious yet poignant true story of the first-ever Jamaican bobsleigh team, who went on to represent their country in the Winter Olympics in Calgary. They are coached by a man called Irv, a former Olympic champion, played by the late John Candy. On arrival in Canada, the team discover that many of the other coaches react negatively to Irv because he had been previously banned for cheating as an athlete.

On the night before their big race, Derice, the captain of the team, confronts Irv and asks him why he had cheated all those years ago. After all, he had already won five gold medals – hadn't he, legitimately, achieved enough?

Irv responds, 'I'd made winning my whole life. And when you make winning your whole life, you have to keep on winning, no matter what ...'

By building his identity on the foundation of success, Irv just had to keep winning – even though it would cost him his reputation and his friends. He goes on to explain that the problem with building your identity on such a thing is that, even when you get it, it still won't be enough. 'A gold medal is a wonderful thing,' he explains, 'but if you're not enough without one, you'll never be enough with one.'[108]

So is there anything on which we can safely build our identity? Something that will not disappoint, and that won't lead us to alienate others or to destroy ourselves in trying to get it?

Transforming our identity

Behind many of our struggles with our identity might be a sense of dissatisfaction with how we feel about ourselves and a sense of dissonance within. We may feel that if we could change some aspect of ourselves, then these feelings would go away. Yet perhaps these feelings are symptomatic of our need for an even more fundamental change to our identity,

Zacchaeus' encounter with Jesus had an instant and transformative effect on his life. He immediately gave away half of his wealth and promised to repay four times the amount to anyone he had cheated. Such actions would have left him considerably less wealthy than before. What brought about this change? Jesus explains, 'Today salvation has come to this house, because this man, too, is a son of Abraham. For the Son of Man came to seek and to save the lost.'[109]

The story began with Zacchaeus being identified by his wealth. It ends with Jesus identifying him as a 'son of Abraham'. While this title may sound alien to us, it would have been highly significant to Zacchaeus and to all those listening to Jesus. In the Bible, being a 'son of Abraham' meant being a part of God's chosen people. Zacchaeus had faced rejection by his own people because of what he had done, yet Jesus wanted him to know clearly that he was now accepted.

As I have already said, Zacchaeus, in many ways, deserved the rejection he experienced. In fact, the Bible goes further, elsewhere saying that he, and we too, deserve rejection by God. We, like Zacchaeus, so often push God to the side of our lives, while building them on other things. Incredibly, despite our rejection of God, he chooses not to reject us. Hanging on the cross, Jesus faced the ultimate rejection for us as he took upon himself all the consequences of what we have done and the way we have lived. Jesus was willing to face the rejection that we deserve so that we can now be accepted. This is what the Bible means when it speaks of *salvation*.

Experiencing the salvation of Jesus means that we too can have a new identity. Our new lives are defined by the fact that we are now connected to Jesus, and that we are known and loved by him.

Embracing our identity

This does not mean that all other aspects of our identity become insignificant. Our identity is multi-faceted, with many things making up who we are. However, being a Christian does mean that the foundation of our identity is now in Jesus, and this makes a real difference.

Firstly, building our identity upon our relationship with Jesus gives us stability. Building our identity on any other foundation proves very unstable and ultimately won't last. A career will end with either redundancy or retirement. Marriages will end with divorce or death. Wealth can be lost. Success can be temporary. However, wonderfully, being known and loved by Jesus gives us a solid and secure foundation that can never be taken away, not even by death. It gives us stability and security throughout the changing seasons of life.

This security can also liberate us to discover and embrace other aspects of who we are, rather than spend time wishing that we were someone else. There may be many ways in which we wish that we could be different, but some of these are outside of our control, as we have already seen. Perhaps Zacchaeus wished he was taller; maybe he had even been ridiculed for his height.

Sometimes, our dissatisfaction with our identity comes from cultural expectations. For instance, we may find that our temperament and natural abilities suit a job in the caring profession rather than in a management role, but society generally considers management more important than those deemed more menial occupations. We can be tempted to feel that our pay grade defines our intrinsic worth. However, trying to force ourselves into a profession or role to which we are not naturally suited will likely only lead to frustration and disappointment. If I know that my identity and value is based on having a relationship with Jesus, it enables me to revaluate all possibilities in the light of this.

Or we may feel the gender we identify as is different to our biological sex. There can be many, and complex, reasons for this. The trans conversation has challenged us to question what gender, sex and sexuality are actually defined as, and how they are connected – or indeed whether they are connected at all. These are huge questions that we haven't space to delve into here.[110]

However, could our questions about our gender identity be, at least sometimes, partly due to our culturally defined expectations of masculinity and femininity? Surprisingly and liberatingly, the Bible's message frees us from such narrow, culturally-constrained views. Instead, it opens up a much wider array of possibilities as to what it means to express our biological sex than 1950s culture would have dreamt possible.

I don't want to suggest that there are simple answers to all our questions about identity, or that becoming a Christian will cause all our identity struggles to go away overnight. However, knowing that the foundation of our identity is based on a relationship with Jesus, who loves us, should at least help us to explore any questions we might have on the subject. The more we realise we are accepted by Jesus, and we develop that stable bond with him, the more secure and at peace we can become. Christians also become part of the church, a community and family in which they can thankfully look *around* and be helped to discover more accurately who they really are – as well as importantly contributing to the formation and development of the given and secure identities of others.

7

Making sense of loneliness

How can we find connection in an isolating world?

In the last twenty years, social commentators had increasingly warned of a growing epidemic. They weren't talking of coronavirus – no one seemed to see that coming – but of an epidemic of loneliness.

Several years before the coronavirus pandemic, the UK had been dubbed the 'loneliness capital of the world'.[111] The government had even appointed a 'Minister for Loneliness' in recognition of the very real and costly problem that loneliness is to society. For instance, it is estimated that lonely people are much more likely to develop serious health problems and are 50% more likely to die prematurely.[112]

While the problem of loneliness among the elderly, particularly the bereaved, has long been recognised, it is loneliness among the young that has gained more recent attention. I was recently speaking at some events in Portugal, where the Christian student movement had been involved in creating a support service for students across the country. The organisation has recently revealed that 25% of the calls they receive are from students struggling with a chronic sense of loneliness.

Interestingly, this increased sense of loneliness correlates with the growing popularity of social media. Studies show that those who use social media the most are also the most likely to say that they feel lonely. While it is unclear whether this is because lonely people are more prone to use social media, or because the platforms increase their loneliness, it would, at least, seem clear that what was designed to bring people together hasn't helped. In fact, it seems to have only increased our sense of missing out and not belonging.

While Covid-19 didn't cause this particular epidemic, it did exacerbate the problem. Lockdowns isolated millions of people from friends and family, imprisoning them in their homes. My own parents were not able to have anyone visit their house for well over a year due to ongoing local restrictions where they live.

Of course, we still had Zoom. We used it for everything, from school and university to birthday parties and 'pub' quizzes. But after the initial novelty had worn off, most people longed for physical connection – not just an internet connection. Interestingly, when news broke of the first successful vaccine, share prices in Zoom crashed, while the share price for airlines took off! We long to be with others – not just on a screen, but in person.

Why are we so lonely?

We might assume that loneliness is a universal, age-old problem. However, in her excellent book *A Biography of Loneliness,* cultural historian Fay Bound Alberti disagrees. She argues that loneliness is a modern emotion and a particular problem today in the West. She explains, 'loneliness in its modern sense emerged as a term and as a recognisable experience around 1800'.[113] Indeed, the English word 'loneliness', with its negative emotional connotations, didn't even exist before then. It wasn't that people were never on their own, but that they didn't perceive it negatively as we do today. She cites two possible reasons for this shift.

First is that the rising acceptance of Darwinian evolution as a way of understanding the world has changed the way we view other people. In a world where only the fittest survive, it is all too easy to go from seeing other people as community to viewing them as competition. Our success depends upon someone else's failure. Second is the decline of religious belief in the West. Up until 1800, it was more common to describe the state of being on one's own as 'solitude' and as a positive thing. So why the difference? Before 1800, it was common for many people in the West to believe in a personal God. Therefore, rather than seeing time alone as a negative thing, it could be viewed as an opportunity to experience, in some way, the presence of God. Being on your own could then serve a positive purpose in bringing you closer to God. Bound Alberti looks at numerous case studies showing how belief in God provided solace and comfort, even in the face of bereavement, loss and isolation.

Is God just a psychological crutch?

The problem for many people in the twenty-first century is that, often, they no longer believe in God – at least, not the personal God revealed in the Bible. While we can see the obvious emotional benefit such a belief might bring in the face of loneliness (and studies have shown the psychological benefits of religious belief[114]), these beliefs might seem little more than having an imaginary friend. Such ideas could be acceptable as a child, but are less fulfilling in adulthood.

But is belief in a personal God who can be present with us at all times simply a psychological crutch, or could it be grounded in reality? To answer that, let's look together at the opening sentences of John's biography of Jesus:

In the beginning was the Word, and the Word was with God, and the Word was God. He was with God in the beginning. Through him all things were made; without him nothing was made that has been made. In him was life, and that life was the light of all mankind. The light shines in the darkness, and the darkness has not overcome it …

The true light that gives light to everyone was coming into the world. He was in the world, and though the world was made through him, the world did not recognise him.

He came to that which was his own, but his own did not receive him. Yet to all who did receive him, to those who believed in his name, he gave the right to become children of God – children born not of natural descent, nor of human decision or a husband's will, but born of God.

The Word became flesh and made his dwelling among us. We have seen his glory, the glory of the one and only Son, who came from the Father, full of grace and truth.[115]

Instead of beginning his biography of Jesus with the story of Jesus' birth in Bethlehem, John goes back much further. He starts at the very beginning of everything, with a deliberate echo of the opening words of Genesis, the first book of the Bible. He talks somewhat cryptically of God as 'the Word' and credits him with the creation of everything.

Such an idea is often quickly dismissed today. Hasn't evolution removed the need for God in regard to the origins of our world? The problem with this assumption, though, is that it overestimates how much evolution can explain. We could ask five big questions about these origins:

1. Why is there anything and not nothing?

2. Why is there order and not chaos?

3. Why is there life, not just lifeless matter?

4. Why is there complex life, not just single cells floating around in a primordial soup?

5. Why is there conscious life, and why do we even read books asking such questions?

Far from answering all of those questions, evolution would, at best, only be able to answer one of them – the fourth one. It cannot answer the others. Indeed, science is often the catalyst to us asking these questions in the first place. For instance, questions two and three have both come about by our *increased* scientific knowledge, not our *lack* of it. The discovery of the beginning and the fine-tuning of the universe raise massive questions, especially for those who don't believe in God.

As Christian author and speaker Glen Scrivener puts it:

Some have spoken of the universe spontaneously creating itself: the whole cosmos propped up by nothing, absolutely nothing. As miracles go this would be unparalleled. Everything from nothing? Christians believe in the virgin birth of Jesus but this would be the virgin birth of the cosmos ... but without a virgin![116]

However, if we want to know whether God exists, and is more than just an illusion or a psychological crutch, then scientific questions can only take us so far. The good news is that John goes further. He continues, 'The Word became flesh and made his dwelling among us. We have seen his glory, the glory of the one and only Son, who came from the Father, full of grace and truth.'[117] John's claim is that the Word who created history has become *part of* history. The Word who created the world has become *part of* his world. And the Word who created humanity has *joined* the human race. The rest of John's book shows us who the Word is: Jesus. In him, God has shown up. This means that our investigation into God can move beyond scientific questions about origins to asking historical questions about a person – Jesus.

Unfortunately, this is often what many well-known atheists fail to do. In seeking to debunk the very idea of God, very few of their arguments focus much attention on Jesus, preferring engagement in philosophical and scientific questions about the origins of the universe. However, Christianity says that the best way to know whether God is really there is to look at Jesus – his historical life, death and resurrection.

John goes on in his book to record Jesus as having made seven astonishing claims about himself. These claims were so outrageous that only someone who believed that he was God could really have made them. For instance, he claimed to be able to forgive sins, that he was the *fulfilment* of history and that he would one day be the *judge* of history. He even used the very name of God from the Old Testament to refer to himself.[118]

Jesus didn't just make great claims, though. (Anyone could do that if they were experiencing hallucinations or disorientation – or were just a downright liar.) Jesus also performed seven great miracles that back up his claims and give force to his words. These culminate in his own crucifixion followed by his resurrection. We will look at this in chapter ten.

For Christians, therefore, the concept of a relatable God is not some psychological crutch, but one that is rooted in the historical claims about Jesus. Yet this leaves a big question: if God's purpose was simply to convince us of his existence, then couldn't he have done it more easily? There are far easier ways of revealing yourself to the world than getting yourself born into an obscure village two millennia ago and then getting executed on a Roman cross. God could convince us of his existence by writing it in the clouds or in the stars. Couldn't he even invite us all to a global Zoom meeting, or perhaps just Zoom-bomb our own meetings?!

However, what if God's purpose was more than simply to convince us that he exists? The historical coming of Jesus shows us that he came to meet our deepest longings and to bring us the connection for which we so long.

Longing for connection

The coronavirus pandemic has made many of us realise how important physical connection is. For a relationship to be truly satisfying, we want to be physically present with the other person. An image on a screen just doesn't compare.

In being born into the world, God showed that he wanted to connect with us. One of the names given to Jesus was 'Immanuel', literally meaning 'God *with* us'.[119]

God didn't just want to convince us that he exists; he desired to establish a relationship with us.

If this is true, how might we respond to such an offer? Verses 11–13 of John chapter 1 show that there are two possible responses we can make: 'He came to that which was his own, but his own did not receive him. Yet to all who did receive him, to those who believed in his name, he gave the right to become children of God – children born not of natural descent, nor of human decision or a husband's will, but born of God.'

Ultimately, we can choose either to reject or to receive this offer with which God reaches out to us.

The choice to reject

It is all too easy to think that the reason we don't believe in God is that we don't have enough evidence. 'If only God would make himself clearer … then we would believe,' we might say. However, it is interesting to note the outcome for some who did meet Jesus physically: they still didn't believe, but chose to reject him. In fact, the Bible says that, explicitly or implicitly, we all do this by nature.[120]

We can easily blame our isolation and loneliness on others. Sometimes this is justified, yet sometimes we must admit that our choices combined with our actions have cut us off from those who love us. While our loneliness might be caused by others' failures to make an effort with us, it could also be due to our failure to do so. Not only can this be the case in our human relationships, but it is certainly the case when it comes to us having any relationship with

God. God created us for connection with himself, but we have often chosen to cut ourselves off from him.

Yet if God is the source of life, light and love, then cutting ourselves off from him is going to be disastrous for us and for our relationships. Like a laptop disconnected from the plug, we can only last so long disconnected from the very source of life. Indeed, our disconnection from God will breed disconnection with each other. Our only focus in a life of disconnection becomes *ourselves*.

A study revealed that video calls are much more tiring than physical meetings with other people. One of the reasons suggested was that on a video call, we spend a high proportion of our time looking at our own image on the screen, rather than directly at the other person. This struck me as somewhat symbolic of the wider realities of our relationship problems. Perhaps we have become too preoccupied with ourselves, and not on others, or on God?

The choice to receive

Thankfully, though, that doesn't have to be the end of the story. Despite our natural default rejection of God, we still have the choice to 'receive' Jesus' offer, and in so doing, to be reconnected in a wonderful way with him. In John's biography of Jesus, this is described as us becoming 'children of God', but what does that mean?

Friends recently adopted a young boy. On the day the adoption was legally established and they took their new son home, he immediately experienced two new truths. Firstly, he had parents who loved him. Secondly, he also acquired siblings who loved him – and who he, too, would learn to love.

The same is true for those who experience what Jesus offers.

1. A Father

Firstly, we can experience the reality of God as a perfect Father. We can enjoy a new father-child relationship with him, although we have done nothing to deserve this. As I described in chapter six, Jesus chose to experience what we actually deserve: rejection by God. He willingly died by crucifixion, and so was cut off from God the Father, for our sake. He faced *ultimate rejection* so that *our* rejection could be forgiven and healed. We have been adopted as children of God. Jesus' subsequent resurrection means that, in a profound way and by his Spirit, he can now be with us at all times and in all places.

For me, this reality has changed the way I see the time when I am alone. Up until the age of thirty-eight, I had been single and had often spent considerable amounts of time on my own. Although there were times when I did feel real loneliness, at other times I was able to see this solitude as a precious opportunity to enjoy my relationship with God as my Father in a deep and tangible way.

2. A family

While being a Christian means that we are brought into our own relationship with God, it would be wrong to assume that we don't need relationships with others too. Permanent solitude is not desirable, even if some Christians think so. Someone who took this idea to the extreme was Simeon Stylites, a fifth-century Syrian monk, who ended up spending thirty-seven years living on a small platform on top of a pillar!

Our need for human connection is revealed in the biblical account of creation. God, having created the first man, says, 'It is not good for the man to be alone.'[121] This may seem surprising given that, at that stage, the man had a good relationship with God – which was far more tangible than ours can currently be – and was living in a very different and perfect world. Surely he had everything he could want? Yet the Bible makes it clear that just as we were made for connection with God, we are also made for connection with other people.

The first human relationship that we see in the Bible is that of marriage. However, the rest of the Bible clarifies that we were also made for other human relationships. These can take many forms as we relate to parents, siblings, children and, not least, friends. It is helpful to note that God did not say, 'It is not good for the man to be unmarried', but rather 'alone'. Marriage alone will not supply all our relational needs. While it is natural to desire marriage, we can still find real and satisfying human connection in other ways, whether or not we are married.

One of the great benefits of receiving Jesus' offer is that it opens up a whole new dynamic of relationship for us to enjoy – that of the church. When we hear the word, 'church', we may instinctively think of an old, grey building, or even, sadly, of an abusive institution – these examples are hardly things that seem beneficial to our emotional wellbeing. Yet according to the Bible, the church is not primarily a building where we go, but a family of which we are part and to which, as Christians, we belong.

I am very thankful for the biological family of which I am a part. They provided me with a stable and loving foundation which has enabled me to flourish. (I am aware that not everyone has had that positive experience.) However, I am also deeply thankful to be part of a Christian family, and that too has been a huge part of my development. It was in large part because of this Christian family that I could enjoy my single years without a crushing sense of loneliness. What is more, wherever in the world I have travelled, I have found members of the church's large, extended family, who have loved and welcomed me. Some of them remain good friends to this day!

I once chatted to a student who had recently decided to start living as a Christian in a part of the world where it is incredibly dangerous to do so. When his family discovered this intention, they threatened to kill him, and he had to flee the country. Yet even though this was so difficult for him, he explained, with a smile on his face, 'I may have lost one family, but I have gained another … and now I have brothers and sisters all over the world.'

A Christian community of people who love God, and who love each other well, is a beautiful place to be. There we can be noticed, valued, accepted, cared for and involved. It is a family that crosses generational, ethnic, cultural, class and gender barriers. It is a place where we can find deep, meaningful connection and belonging. If you've never experienced a Christian community like that, then why not look one up? Why not ask the person who recommended this book to you, or get in touch with me directly?[122]

We live in a world of increasingly isolated and alone humans. However, through Jesus, we can find and receive both a fatherly God who loves us, and a real, present family who care passionately for us and others. In such a community, when the church is functioning at its best, it would be difficult to ever feel deep loneliness. It is designed that way.

8

Making sense of freedom

Will following my heart set me free?

All was calm as I walked across Maidan Square in Kiev in 2015, yet all around me were reminders of what had so recently taken place. Every paving stone had been ripped up and large barricades stood across the adjoining streets. Just a few days before, weeks of mass protests had ended in a bloody massacre, with riot police opening fire on the protestors, before the president finally, and abruptly, fled the country.

Fear, tension and anxiety had now been replaced by a sense of hope at the new-found freedom that the country might be able to enjoy. Sadly, that optimism faded fast when reprisals led to the annexation of Crimea and years of devastating war in the east of the country.

Freedom comes in many different forms. As well as our desire for political freedom, as expressed in many such protests around the world, we have a desire for freedom of speech – the right to express one's views and beliefs without hindrance. Just as political freedom is under threat from authoritarian regimes, many people believe that our freedom of speech is also under threat. Recently, 150 leading academics, writers and activists signed an open letter to that effect.

Closely tied to freedom of speech is freedom of religion – the right to express or change one's religious beliefs. While we westerners tend to take such a freedom for granted, many in the world today do not enjoy this liberty.

Underlying all of these rights is our desire for personal freedom. In my work with students, it is quite clear that, for many undergraduates, attending a university is not just about gaining a qualification. It is also about enjoying freedom away from home and away from the constraints or expectations of the family. They might say they are finally free to be who they want to be.

Our desire for freedom, and the beauty of it, is expressed in many of the greatest films. *The Shawshank Redemption* explores freedom from imprisonment. *Les Misérables* depicts freedom from oppression. *Braveheart* portrays freedom from the English!

Where do we find freedom?

In our search for freedom, I'm guessing many of us wouldn't expect to find it in Christianity. Religion is commonly seen as being about rules and rituals – a list of onerous obligations, and the constant denial or suppression of our desires.

Ned Flanders, from the TV sitcom *The Simpsons,* is a famous Christian cartoon character. In one episode, when pressed as to why he looks so youthful, he reveals that it is actually due to his life of self-denial: 'I resist all the major urges ... No, no, and double no! I haven't done any of those things, folks. You name it, I haven't done it!'

To which Homer replies, 'Jeez, Flanders, you're sixty, and you've never lived a day in your life!'[123]

For many, Christianity seems like the complete antithesis to freedom. Yet while we may not expect to find freedom in a religion, does rejecting God really offer the liberty we desire either?

Many atheists have realised that a consistent outworking of their belief would force them to hold that who we are and what we do is ultimately determined by two factors: our environment and our DNA. In this case, we don't really have free choice, even if we think we do. The political philosopher John Gray put it well when he explained, 'Modern humanism is the faith that, through science, humankind can know the truth – and so be free. But if Darwin's theory of natural selection is true this is impossible. The human mind serves evolutionary success, not truth.'[124] Is that really a freedom worth having? Maybe we need to step back and ask a fundamental question about the nature of freedom.

What even is freedom?

It is easy to assume that freedom is defined as being able to do whatever I want, whenever I want, with whoever

I want, for as long as I want. In other words, freedom means life with no limits and no restrictions. Ever since the Enlightenment, this has been the popular understanding of freedom in the West. However, the following three incidents may help us to see that there is more to freedom than simply doing what we like.

Shortly after returning from a trip to New Zealand, I was struck by a news item from that country. Hundreds of pilot whales had become stranded on a beach in the north of South Island. Despite the heroic efforts of hundreds of locals, many of them sadly perished. Is a whale on the beach free? Of course not. Whales are only free in the ocean. Within the vast, rich ocean, they can swim for thousands of miles without hindrance. On a beach, without rescue, the stark fact is that they will soon be dead. In a similar way, are there limits to *our* freedom? Could there be ways when 'doing whatever I want' leads us not to freedom, but to the exact opposite – our ruin?

The second incident was on my long journey home from New Zealand, when I watched the movie *Frozen*. I thought it might help me to acclimatise back to a northern hemisphere winter! In the film, the main character, Elsa, is fed up with having to conceal her abilities and desires to be free. So she cuts loose, leaves home and sets up her own ice castle. However, while she is now free to do what she wants, her expression of freedom has left her alone. She then comes to discover that neither can she really be free: 'Oh I'm such a fool' because there is 'No escape from the storm inside of me'.[125] In the same way, by desiring freedom, could we end up cutting ourselves off from those who know and love us, rendering us soberingly alone?

Keeping with the icy theme, the third incident that taught me much about freedom happened a number of years previously, when I first learnt to ski. At the time, I was dating a girl who lived in America, and whose parents had generously paid for me to join them on their annual ski holiday in Colorado. The only problem was that they went skiing every year, while I had never been skiing in my life! In an effort not to embarrass myself, I decided to get three hours of lessons on a dry ski slope before I went.

My instructor spent most of the time teaching me how to control my speed and stop. I wasn't much interested in stopping, which seemed tedious. I wanted to be able to go! I watched the experienced skiers whizz down the main slope and just wanted to be free to do the same.

Once in America, I was excited to get going on a proper mountain, free from my instructor's continual desire to restrain me. However, as we went up in the lofty chairlift, it suddenly dawned on me that this mountain was quite a bit bigger and steeper than that dry ski slope. As I disembarked from the lift, I started to slide slowly across the open area at the top of the mountain, displaying little control. My first thought was that I needed to stop, do my ski boots up properly and wait for the rest of the family. There was only one problem: I couldn't stop.

Initially, I wasn't travelling fast as the gradient was very gentle. However, I soon realised that I was heading for the start of the main red run. Before I could do anything about it, I was descending it, picking up speed as I went. As I got faster and faster, I desperately tried to remember how to stop ...

Even if you have never been skiing before, you can work out that one way to stop very quickly is to fall over. In my pride, I thought that would be embarrassing. I wanted to find another way. At that moment, an idea popped into my head. Off the edge of the piste was a forest. I figured if I could just ski into the forest, I could grab hold of one of the trees and stop myself. So off I went towards the forest, through deep snow, off-piste.

The stupidity of this idea became evident to me very quickly as I hit the first tree, head on, at high speed. Moments later, I was lying flat on my back, embedded in white, with both skis off, bruises from head to toe and an anxious family looking down at me.

'What were you trying to do?!' my girlfriend asked.

'I was trying to stop,' I explained.

'Didn't they teach you how to stop?!' her dad asked, exasperated.

'Yes,' I responded, 'but I didn't listen to that part of the lesson.'

'Well, if you can't remember how to stop in future, then just fall over!' they exclaimed.

So that is what I did for the rest of the day, repeatedly. In fact, I made such slow progress that, by nightfall, I was still only halfway down the mountain and had to be taken down the remainder on the back of a Ski-Doo.

The following day, her parents paid for me to get some lessons and I finally did learn how to stop. For the next week, I flew down every mountain in the resort in a crazy snowplough posture, trying to make up for lost time. It didn't work. A few weeks later, my girlfriend ended the relationship. A month later, I heard she was dating a ski instructor. Before the year was out, she had married him!

I don't recount the story to gain your pity. I am now happily married and I have even learnt to ski properly. But the experience did teach me something about freedom. I thought I was free when I got to the mountain because I had no one to tell me what to do. But, actually, I wasn't in control; gravity was! And gravity was going to take me wherever it wanted. If we are not really in control of what we do, can we really claim to be free?

Could it be that our contemporary concepts of freedom are too simplistic? Could there be fresh wisdom to be gained from an ancient approach? One of the most profound statements on freedom comes from antiquity: 'You will know the truth, and the truth will set you free.' It surprises many people to discover these words were actually spoken by Jesus. We may not ordinarily think that Jesus has much to tell us about freedom, but let's take a deeper look.

Jesus and freedom

Jesus said, 'If you hold to my teaching, you are really my disciples. Then you will know the truth, and the truth will set you free.'

> *They answered him, 'We are Abraham's descendants*
> *and have never been slaves of anyone. How can you say*
> *that we shall be set free?'*
>
> *Jesus replied, 'Very truly I tell you, everyone who sins*
> *is a slave to sin. Now a slave has no permanent place in*
> *the family, but a son belongs to it for ever. So if the Son*
> *sets you free, you will be free indeed.'*[126]

Jesus originally spoke these words to a group of respected religious leaders. They find Jesus' words offensive. By saying that they need to be set free, Jesus is implying that they *aren't* free at that moment. They respond angrily, insisting that they don't need to be set free because they have never been slaves.

These are, perhaps, some of the most ironic words in the Bible. The history of the nation of Israel ('Abraham's descendants', of which these people were a part) is littered with their enslavement – firstly by the Egyptians; then by the Assyrians, Babylonians and Persians; and, more recently, by the Greeks. As Jesus speaks, they are living under Roman occupation. So much for being free!

Yet interestingly, while Jesus could have pointed out their obvious need for political freedom, he goes on to explain he is not talking about this kind of freedom. Indeed, it is quite possible to be politically free but still to be enslaved in a different way.

We are not free

Jesus explains that none of us are actually free. He describes us as being slaves to sin. When we hear the word 'sin', we may be tempted to think of the forbidden and frivolous, but in the Bible, sin would appear to go *far* deeper.

One writer described sin as the 'universal human propensity to f**k things up'.[127] It is the instinctive bias in each one of us that means that, so often, we are our own worst enemy. We have a self-destructive side to our human nature. We are like a shopping trolley that seems to go any way other than the way it should.

The singer-songwriter John Mayer describes it well in his song 'Gravity',[128] singing of the way he keeps self-destructing in his relationships and throwing away what he has. Just as with gravity, sin is like an unseen force that continually drags us down.

Jesus' metaphor of slavery is helpful here. We can easily see how some addictions – such as drugs, alcohol, sex and gambling – can enslave people and destroy their lives. But what if we were *all* enslaved, in some way?

Russell Brand's book *Recovery* describes his journey out of alcohol and drug addiction. I was struck by his comment at the start: 'Those of us born with clear-cut and blatant substance addiction are in many ways the lucky ones. We alcoholics and junkies have minimized the mystery to tiny circles of craving and fulfilment. Our pattern is easier to observe and therefore, with commitment and help, easier to resolve.'[129]

He goes on to explain that all of us look to material things in one form or another to fulfil us, and that these things, eventually, will disappoint. It is easy to see that drugs can never satisfy. It can take longer to realise that foreign holidays, a successful career, a happy family and a bigger house will also fail to give us what we ultimately need. All of us are enslaved.

We can be enslaved by our phones – spending up to a quarter of our lives in front of our screens.[130] But what do we really hope to find as we scroll down our social media feed for the hundredth time today? We can possibly be enslaved by a career – sacrificing our time, relationships and even our health to get on. We can be enslaved by our peers – doing things we don't want to do, in an effort to be liked and accepted. We can be enslaved by our desires – having to do whatever our impulses tell us, even if we know we might regret this in time.

If we take the time to seriously think about it, we might come to realise that we are not as free as we thought … But, thankfully, that doesn't have to be the end of the story. Freedom is possible!

Jesus can set us free

Jesus' words in the passage imply that none of us are, by nature, free. Yet in the same breath, Jesus reveals that he is the one who is able to set us free. Jesus never diagnoses our problems without also offering a solution. Jesus can set us free in these ways.

Freedom from guilt

Günter Grass was a much-celebrated German novelist and poet who won the Nobel Prize in literature. In his 2006 autobiography, *Peeling the Onion,* he made a shocking revelation about his earlier life that had remained hidden for sixty years. Despite spending much of his career criticising Germany's failure to deal with its Nazi past, he admitted in his book that he had himself been part of the Nazi SS during the war. Many criticised him for his hypocrisy. He was asked why he chose to reveal the truth at that point, after so many years. He simply admitted, 'It had to come out', while also recognising that 'it will stain me forever'.[131]

All of us have done, said and thought things that, if made public, would stain us too. We may not have been violent fascists, but we have made decisions that have hurt others and have had a destructive impact upon their lives and ours. We can end up carrying around a sense of regret, guilt and shame. Even if we choose to conceal these things, as so many of us do, the burden of doing so can be exhausting.

That is why Jesus' offer of forgiveness is so liberating. With forgiveness comes freedom from guilt and shame, but that freedom is costly. Just as our political freedom was bought at the cost of the lives of others, so our ultimate freedom came only through Jesus' bloody death for us on the cross. He chose to *lose* his freedom so that we might find it. By his death, he took upon himself all our guilt and shame so that we could be freed from it. He offers us the freedom of a completely fresh start.

On a trip to Bosnia, I met Saša, who told me his story. He revealed that during the war in the former Yugoslavia, he had killed many people. After the war, racked with a sense of guilt for what he had done, his life spiralled downwards – until he met a team of Romanian Christians who had come to his town. He was drawn to them by their joy, and through them, heard of the offer of Jesus' forgiveness. He responded by putting his own trust in Jesus, and so experienced a sense of forgiveness that was to be life-changing. 'My guilt melted away like the snow in the springtime,' he explained, 'and I could sleep for the first time in years.'

If Jesus can offer this kind of forgiveness to Saša, then we too can be set free from our guilt.

Freedom from humanity's destructive side

The freedom that Jesus brings is not simply from the guilt of our sin, but also from its power. We can be liberated from our self-destructive nature.

I love flying, so it is great being married to a pilot. My favourite part of a flight is always the take-off. As I sat downstairs in the jumbo jet that she was about to pilot to Cape Town, I suddenly wondered how much a Boeing 747 weighs. It must be a lot – and even more so when we were all sitting in it, along with our luggage. How was this thing ever going to get into the air? But within a few moments, we were rushing down the runway; seconds later, we were in the air. Then another thought came to my mind. How much does this plane weigh now? And the scary truth was exactly the same as it did a few moments before. So how were we now in the air, and had not crashed onto the motorway at the end of the runway? The answer is that while the force of gravity was still pulling the plane down, a greater force was now lifting it up.

In the same way, Jesus is able to give us new power in our lives. We may still face the temptation to do stuff that we know is not ultimately right or good for us, but, by his Spirit, God gives us the strength to live differently and to make different choices. We are not left to pull ourselves up by our own shoelaces; our own moral efforts alone are not enough to change our life. But by relying upon the help that Jesus gives, real and lasting change is possible in our lives.

A few years ago, I had the joy of meeting Tom Tarrants. Several decades before, Tom had been one of America's most wanted terrorists. During his arrest, he had been shot multiple times and left for dead. As we sat and chatted in a pleasant study in Oxford, it was hard to imagine what he must have previously been like. During his second imprisonment (he had escaped and been recaptured), he started reading the Bible and had a life-changing encounter with Jesus. As the title of his autobiography explains, a life that had been consumed by hate had now been redeemed by love.[132]

If Jesus has the power to set someone like Tom free, then he can also give us the power we need to become the people who, in our best moments, we really want to be. This does not mean that we won't ever fail, or that this new life of freedom will be easy. While Jesus sets us free from the destructive power of sin, we are not totally free from the presence and influence of the broken world in which we live. Just as gravity will continue to act against an aeroplane in the air, so we will still have to do battle with our own self-destructive desires.

In fact, becoming a Christian may, at least at first, make us *more aware* of them! The other day, I went swimming down the River Thames outside our house. I wasn't aware of the current as I swam with it (I just thought I was swimming fast!). It was only when I turned round and tried to swim upstream that I suddenly became aware of its speed. Likewise, Jesus wants to empower us to go against the flow of our own destructive desires – and certain aspects of our own culture. The more we experience true freedom, the more we won't want to be pulled back into our former life of slavery.

Freedom to be who we were made to be

The film *The Shawshank Redemption* explores what it means to really be free. Set in a high-security prison, the film follows the lives of a number of prisoners. One of the older inmates, a man called Brooks, has been behind bars for much of his life. When he is finally released, we see his struggle to adapt to the changed world in which he now finds himself. Alone, and without purpose, he tragically ends up taking his own life. This fires Andy, one of the other inmates, not only to work to free his friend Red, but also to go to great lengths to prepare a life he can fit into once he is no longer behind bars.

True freedom is not simply about being freed *from* something, but also about being set free *for* something. We need to have something or someone to live for. Jesus not only frees us from the guilt and power of sin, but also brings us back into relationship with God himself. It is in that relationship of love that we are free to be who we were uniquely made to be.

The artist Michelangelo is perhaps most famous for his sculpture of David, the biblical shepherd and then king. If you go to the Accademia Gallery in Florence to view this work, you will also see a series of other sculptures that appear unfinished. The figures seem to remain imprisoned in their blocks of marble. However, it has been suggested that Michelangelo deliberately left them in this state to illustrate the human struggle for freedom. They may also have reflected his own experience. It was only later in Michelangelo's life that he came to discover Jesus in a more personal and transformative fashion, leading him to experience what it meant to be truly free.

Freedom to choose

Jesus came to set us free from that which ultimately would destroy our lives so that we can live in abundant relationship with God. Yet because being a Christian is about having such a relationship with God, it also involves the freedom to choose. Love doesn't force; it must allow the loved one a freedom to choose their response. In the same way, God gives us the freedom to choose how to respond to his deep love for us. No one can be forced to be a Christian! It is a choice for us all to make.

This understanding of real love, which is at the heart of Christianity, explains why freedom, in all its many forms, has been one of the obvious consequences of the Christian revolution. It is no accident that there is a strong correlation between the influence of Christianity around the world and the prevalence not only of religious freedom, but also of political freedom and the freedom of speech.

Living in the West, we enjoy many of these freedoms. However, have we yet discovered the deep freedom from which they originated? Do we know the freedom of forgiveness? Do we have an identifiable knowledge of freedom with God?

9

Making sense of love

Why is love so important yet so hard to find?

One of the joys of long-distance travel is watching movies that I meant to go and see at the cinema, but never got around to seeing. On a recent trip, I watched two movies that turned out to be strikingly similar.

Bohemian Rhapsody tells the story of the troubled musical genius Freddie Mercury, while *Rocketman* focuses on the upbringing and early career of Elton John. Both achieved great musical success. Yet both also had painful and difficult relationships with their fathers, faced rejection because of their sexuality and struggled with addictions of various kinds. Ultimately, behind both stories is the search for love. Freddie Mercury once commented, 'You can have everything in the world and still be the loneliest man, and this is the most bitter type of loneliness … Success has brought me world idolisation and millions of pounds, but it has prevented me from experiencing what we all need – a loving, on-going relationship.'[133]

I found myself deeply moved at the pain and rejection that both men had experienced, and at the way they had suffered through being used by others. Many others who have achieved great success or significance have similarly struggled to experience the love they so desperately desire. While still incredibly popular and successful, Robbie Williams sang, 'I just want to feel real love'[134] and revealed his longings for acceptance and belonging. Shortly before her tragic and premature death, Diana, Princess of Wales spoke movingly of her loneliness and pain. Despite being known and admired by millions, she felt alone.

These examples reveal that our search in life is not so much for some*thing*, but for some*one*. It is not, after all, what we *have*, but who we are *with* that makes the biggest difference in life. We can accumulate much, but if we don't experience real love, there is the sense that something is missing. Out of all our human desires, the desire for love is the most powerful.

Yet we don't have to achieve world idolisation or possess millions of pounds to know that love is more important than even the best material things. Love, particularly romantic love, can bring life's greatest joy; the absence of love can lead to life's greatest pain.

What is love?

After giving a talk on the Christian faith in a Danish university, I got chatting to a student and asked her what she had thought of it. She responded by saying, simply and bluntly, 'I wasn't interested. I'm not into God.'

I respected her honesty. Most British students wouldn't be so direct! Yet I was also keen to continue the conversation, so I asked, 'What *are* you into?' I'm well aware that many people are not interested in God – or at least the concept of God with which they have grown up, but I am yet to find someone who isn't interested in *anything*!

'I'm into love,' she replied.

'What would you say love actually *is*?' I probed.

She thought deeply for a few moments. 'I'm not sure,' she finally concluded.

'Can I give you a definition of love?' I enquired.

She nodded, so I continued, 'Love is the chemical reaction that has evolved in our brains to make us attracted to people, typically of the opposite sex, so that we reproduce and pass on our DNA.'

'That's not love!' she retorted (possibly because her boyfriend was sitting next to her).

'Why not?' I persisted.

Again, she thought for a few moments before concluding, 'I'm not sure.'

If there is no God, and if we live in a materialistic universe where there is nothing more than physical matter, it is hard to explain why love should be anything more than my definition above.

Patricia Churchland, a Canadian-American neuro-philosopher, was very consistent with her atheistic beliefs when she said, 'The principal chore of brains is to get the body parts where they should be in order that the organism may survive ... a fancier style of representing [the world] is advantageous so long as it ... enhances an organism's chances for survival.'[135] Is love nothing more than a way of ensuring that we continue to propagate our DNA? If this is the case, then what do we say of those who continue to love someone even when such propagation is not possible? Richard Dawkins, the celebrated atheistic thinker, explained these feelings in this way:

> We can no more help ourselves feeling pity when we see a weeping unfortunate (who is unrelated and unable to reciprocate) than we can help ourselves feeling lust for a member of the opposite sex (who may be infertile or otherwise unable to reproduce). Both are misfirings, Darwinian mistakes: blessed, precious mistakes.[136]

Is that all love is in such instances? A mistake? A misfiring of the evolutionary process?

Think about it a different way. 'The anatomical juxtaposition of two orbicularis oris muscles in a state of contraction' is the scientific definition of a kiss, but is that *all* a kiss is?

I was recently in Belarus and noticed a particular song, 'Endorfina', was frequently being played on the radio. A friend translated the lyrics, which clearly, like many love songs, had been written in a moment of painful rejection. But it was the refrain that struck me. The singer Max Korzh asks why, if his feelings are just the release of endorphins or the explosion of oxytocin, do they hurt so much?[137]

This illustrates the problem with a reductionist worldview – one that reduces everything in the universe down to chemical processes and explains everything away as the behaviour of atoms and molecules. Ultimately, the philosophy explains away some of the most precious, profound parts of life.

One response is not to think too deeply about anything, for fear that we will be forced to challenge our own conclusions. We could just get on and enjoy love without wondering what love is, but is there another way that takes seriously our deepest emotions and accounts for them with integrity?

In my conversation with the Danish student, she then asked me, 'So what do *you* think love is?'

I responded by explaining that actually I thought love had quite a lot to do with God.

'How so?' she asked.

I went on to explain that, according to the Bible, God *is* love.[138] Love is not just something he does from time to time; it is who he fundamentally *is*. His very nature is love.

This, of course, raises another question: if God is love, then how was God love before there was anyone *to* love? If God was around before us, before the world or before anything else, how could God still be love? Love surely requires an object of affection?

This is one reason why a worldview such as Islam would struggle to account for a God of love. In such a belief system, God is on his own – a singularity. Who did God love when there was nothing but God?

However, it is not a problem in the Christian faith – indeed, it taps into one of the most fundamental things about who God is. Christian theologians use the word 'Trinity' to explain that God is actually multi-personal and relational. The Bible talks about God the Father, God the Son and God the Spirit – three distinct persons, each fully God, but united as *one* by their love for each other. The best symbol we have for depicting this is marriage, where husband and wife are united as 'one flesh'.[139] The Spice Girls were perhaps unknowingly quoting the Bible when they sang, 'two become one'.[140] God *can* be love because God has always been in a loving relationship.

This understanding of the incredible self-giving love of God is significant because the Bible tells us God created human beings 'in his image'.[141] So if the most important thing about God is that he is love, then surely the most important aspect about being human is that we are made for love: to love and to be loved. The Beatles were more correct than they knew when they sang, 'All you need is love' all those years ago!

The search for a deeper love

The Danish student thought for a moment about my definition of love before responding, 'So if love is so important, then why is it so hard to find?' It was a very good question.

Perhaps the best way to answer it is by looking at another of Jesus' encounters. On this occasion, Jesus meets a woman who is thirsty. She has come to a well in the midday heat to get water. But we also get the impression, from how the conversation unfolds, that she has a deeper thirst too: a thirst for love, for acceptance and for belonging. Just as she was getting water to quench her physical thirst, it would seem that she has been looking to *marriage* to quench her deeper thirst. In fact, we discover that she has been married five times ... and is now living with another man.[142]

We aren't told any of the details of what happened, but we can imagine what *might* have occurred. Think back a few years. She's got it all planned out: the wedding dress, the bridesmaids and the flowers. All this ... and she's only five! Fast forward a few years and she finally meets the guy she's been waiting for. They fall madly in love, and after a whirlwind romance, he proposes. After the wedding of their dreams, they settle down together and everything seems great – for a while. Then it all goes wrong. Before long, she's on her own again.

Then she meets another guy. 'Now this is the man,' she thinks to herself. He appears to be everything the first guy wasn't, in so many ways. They soon get married, and again everything is great – for a while. But then that marriage ends too.

She then meets number three. 'Third time lucky!' perhaps she thinks to herself. But that one also comes to an end.

As does the next.

And the next.

Finally, when she meets number six, she thinks, 'Why bother marrying? It's not going to last. Let's save ourselves some hassle and just live together.'

Now here she is, alone, with her shattered dreams and broken promises. The reality of life has been so far from her past expectations. We too experience this huge gulf between our expectation of love and its reality.

On the one hand, our society still maintains a deeply romantic ideal of love – one that will conquer every fear, overcome every barrier and satisfy every need. It is the love we see portrayed in films and sung about in songs. Consider how strange it would be if you heard a love song proclaim, 'I'll love you for … quite a long time', or, 'I'll love you with … most of my heart'! We instinctively feel that love should be all-consuming, absolute and for ever.

However, the reality of life can teach us otherwise. Chris Martin and Gwyneth Paltrow were widely regarded as having one of the more successful celebrity marriages, before – to the surprise of many – they separated. Instead of talking of divorce, they described it as a 'conscious uncoupling' and explained that it was unreasonable to expect marriage should last a lifetime now that people are living longer.

The painful experiences of life can leave us sceptical or even cynical about the more romantic expectations of love. We don't have to have been married at all, let alone five times, to know that love doesn't always last and, even at its best, doesn't always satisfy in the way that we might have hoped. Maybe you too can identify with the painful experience of disappointment that this woman must have felt.

We aren't told how her relationships began or how they ended. The husbands might all have died or might have been unfaithful. Societal pressure may have forced her, against her will, into marriages that were unloving or abusive. Alternatively, she may have played her own part in the demise of the relationships.

The reality is that sometimes relationships end because of the brokenness of our world; no one is to blame. For example, I met a couple who discovered they were expecting their first child, but soon also learnt that Tim had a brain tumour. He lived long enough to see the birth of his daughter, Imogen, but not long enough for her to have any living memories of him. Sometimes, though, our pain is directly the result of how others have treated us. We become the innocent victims of their selfish and destructive choices. At other times, we can be responsible for the breakdown of our relationships. It is often painful to live with the consequences of our own choices and the wish we had chosen differently.

A surprising encounter

Not only does Jesus walk into this woman's situation, but the fact that he does so at all is quite surprising when we know a little about the geography and culture of the situation.

The incident takes place while Jesus is on a journey north to the region of Galilee. We read that en route 'he *had*' to go through a region called Samaria. From a purely geographical point of view, this was strange as there was a more direct route. What is more, most Jews would have avoided the region (ethnic conflict in the Middle East is sadly nothing new). We see this in the way that the woman responds to Jesus' request for a drink. She exclaims, 'You are a Jew and I am a Samaritan woman. How can you ask me for a drink?'[143]

It is not just her ethnicity and gender that would have caused this woman to be surprised by Jesus' interest in her. In addition, her failed marriages, plus her choice to live with someone to whom she wasn't married, would have caused her to be ostracised by those in her own community. Indeed, this is probably why she is out alone in the midday sun getting water – avoiding the cooler times of day when she would be more likely to have to interact with others.

Jesus is willing to cross these geographical, cultural, ethnic and religious barriers to meet her. How does he then respond to her? We might naturally expect him to condemn her for her life choices. Isn't that what religious leaders can sometimes do, stating how far wrong we have gone? Maybe you have been made to feel even worse about your own situation by the uncaring and condemning attitude of others. But that is not the attitude of Jesus.

Conversely, maybe we would expect Jesus to condone her actions, saying that everything is fine and it really doesn't matter how she lives. Five husbands? No problem! We perhaps like the idea of a religion that makes no

is he? It is only at the end of the encounter that Jesus reveals the answer.

After Jesus shows an astonishing, and seemingly supernatural, ability to know details about the woman's life, we see her response: 'Sir ... I can see that you are a prophet ... I know that Messiah (called Christ) is coming. When he comes, he will explain everything to us.'[147] Jesus then declares, 'I, the one speaking to you – I am he.'[148]

Both Jews and Samaritans shared the hope that, one day, God would send someone to put right our disordered world and heal our broken lives. Jesus' remarkable response is that *he is that person*! In fact, by referring to himself here and elsewhere as 'I am', he is not just claiming to be *sent* from God, but to *be* God. Jesus can meet our deepest needs because he is *far more than* we might initially think he is.

2. What he has done

Jesus' meeting with the woman is not the only occasion in this biographical account of Jesus' life where someone is thirsty. Later on in John's account, we read of how Jesus was crucified to death on a cross, which was an excruciatingly painful experience – literally. While hanging on the cross, one of the few things that Jesus is recorded as saying is, 'I thirst.' We know that those crucified experienced physical thirst, but why does Jesus only express his thirst and not the many other deeply painful aspects of crucifixion?

It would seem that even at the height of physical agony, Jesus is referring to something deeper than just physical thirst. He is experiencing the deeper relational and spiritual thirst that each one of us experiences. On the cross, Jesus is experiencing the ultimate thirst that comes from the aloneness of abandonment – not just by his followers who loved him, but, in a profound way, by God the Father. Jesus does this so that *our* deep thirst for eternal life and love might be quenched. His own relationship with God the Father was broken so that *ours* with him could be restored. Jesus can offer us the ultimate of all relationships because he gave his own up for us, out of his perfect, unfailing love.

This may still leave you with questions about what it is actually like to experience the love of God in Jesus. Does it mean that we spend our lives with a warm, fuzzy feeling of love hanging around that never goes away? Your experience of other Christians may confirm that this isn't the case ... So is God's love really as good as I am making out, or is Jesus guilty of overstating what he offers?

It is important to notice that Jesus says that the water he offers will 'well up' to eternal life. It's an experience that can start now, today even, but will continue on and on, as does water from a well. It is wonderful to really know the love of God today. It is great to know his presence in your life. Yet the Bible points to a day when it will be *even better*. We could say the imagery of the Bible is that being a Christian, here and now, is a bit like the state of being engaged – Christians are still waiting for the anticipated wedding day! Having recently got married, I can confirm that, while it was great being engaged, it is far better being married. The Bible says that some of our longings and desires will start to be met now, as we experience more of God's love in Jesus for ourselves. Importantly, though, we can also look forward to a day when our longings for true love will be *fully* met, *for ever*.

Earlier, we spoke of God as an eternally loving relationship between the Father, Son and Spirit. The wonder of the Christian story is that we get invited to become part of that amazing relationship of love.

Another question that we might ask is: if God's love is so all-satisfying, do we still need human love? Why do we still long for human relationships and intimacy? These desires are not wrong. We are made to have human relationships. At the very beginning of the Bible, when the first man was in a perfect world and enjoying a perfect relationship with his Creator, God still said, 'It is not good for the man to be alone'[149] and therefore created a companion for him.

Knowing the love of God doesn't remove the need for us to experience love from others in different ways, but it does remove the unrealistic expectation that their love will fully satisfy us and complete us. It also means that we become connected to the very source of love, God himself, who *is* love. As a result, we can find ourselves better able to love each other. Instead of loving others in the hope that they will repay us with their love, we can love others even when they don't – for we have already experienced love that will never fail, giving us a confident security. Knowing the love of God doesn't mean that we will love other people less, but that we will love them far, far better.

10

Making sense of hope

How can we find freedom from fear?

On a cold December morning, a US Navy submarine, USS S-4, surfaced near Cape Cod, just off the north-east coast of America. It reached the surface at the very same moment that a Coast Guard destroyer happened to be passing by. The destroyer had no time to change course and rammed the submarine, which immediately sank to the ocean floor. A desperate rescue effort was launched to see if anyone trapped inside was still alive. The team of divers sent down could hear the sound of tapping coming from the hull. It was morse code. The message, repeated again and again, was simply this: 'Is . there . any . hope?'

It's a good question.

Is there any hope?

When we look out at our world, we could ask the same question. As we see society becoming increasingly polarised, or observe a growing environmental crisis, or witness yet more conflict, inequality and injustice, it can cause us to wonder whether there is any hope.

We may also ask the same question as we look in at our own lives. As we struggle with questions of our own identity, or as we battle with a sense of isolation and loneliness, or as we wrestle with our own pain, it can make us ask if there is any reason to have hope.

Hope seems so hard to find. In fact, while we live in a society that seems to be divided on many issues, the one thing that appears to unite us is a sense of fear and panic about what might happen tomorrow. Whatever your political persuasion and personal views, fear of the future is a common human denominator. The only variants are of *what* each of us is fearful.

Should we despair?

In many of the culturally divisive issues of the last few years, those taking opposing sides have often been motivated out of a fear of what will happen otherwise.

During the coronavirus pandemic, many people were very fearful of the direct threat of Covid-19 upon their health and that of others, as well as being fearful about their national health service's ability to cope with the pandemic. As a result, they pressed for *greater* restrictions. Others were less fearful of the physical health risks, but instead were fearful of the mental and emotional health risks that lockdown and isolation can bring. They were also fearful for the long-term health of the economy – not just in regard to their own jobs, but also with regard to their country as a whole. As a result, they pressed for an *easing* of lockdown restrictions.

During the debates that surrounded the UK leaving the European Union, a great deal of fear was expressed by both sides. Many of those who wanted to stay part of the EU expressed a fear of what would happen if we didn't remain within the EU – including possible financial disaster and increased political instability across the continent. However, others who voted to leave expressed fear about what would happen if we stayed in the European Union – including a fear of growing authoritarianism and uncontrolled immigration.

Fear was a big factor in recent American elections. Many voters seemed to be fearful about what would happen if the opposition party got into power. They therefore voted not so much because they were convinced by the quality of their own particular candidate, but rather out of fear and dislike of the other one.

Debates about issues of racial justice have also involved fear. On the one hand, there is fear of a growing resurgence in racism and the harm this could cause to certain groups. On the other, there is a fear of what would happen if such things as the demand to 'defund the police' were actually implemented.

Likewise, much of the debate around environmental issues is prompted by fear. On the one hand, there is a genuine fear of an impending environmental disaster if we don't make a significant dent in our global carbon emissions. Perhaps the clearest articulation of this kind of fear was expressed by Greta Thunberg, the climate activist, in a speech during the World Economic Forum in Davos. She challenged the assembled world leaders by saying categorically, 'I don't want you to be hopeful. I want you to panic. I want you to feel the fear I feel every day. And then I want you to act.'[150] On the other hand, some deny that climate change is even real, motivated by a fear that some hidden political agenda is being smuggled in under the auspices of environmental concern.

Why do we speak so much about fear and panic? Maybe it is because many of us, like Greta, believe the only way to get people to act is if they are fearful. We all seem to be fearful of the future, though of different threats. However, as we saw in chapter two, being motivated primarily by fear brings problems.

One problem is the temptation to overstate your case in an attempt to gain more attention for your cause. It is all too common to predict disaster if people don't act in the way that you think they should. Yet while there often is a very real case to be made, overstating it can actually lead to the issue being undermined once evidence to the contrary arises, or when the predicted disaster doesn't happen.

However, one of the biggest problems with being motivated by fear is that it doesn't always lead to positive and lasting change, but rather to panicked, knee-jerk reactions. While the passion and conviction it displays may be admirable, there is growing evidence that staying in a state of heightened emotional distress not only adversely affects our own longer-term mental and emotional health, but actually diminishes our ability to act in constructive ways. The Australian Psychological Society provides this advice: 'Although environmental threats are real and can be frightening, remaining in a state of heightened distress is not helpful for ourselves or for others. We generally cope better, and are more effective at making changes, when we are calm and rational.'[151]

This can be evidenced by watching the different ways in which my wife and I drive a car. If I get lost or take the wrong turning, I am far more likely to panic and compound one mistake with yet more. For my wife, years of training as an airline pilot has taught her how to respond better in such situations. A calm but clear awareness of the problem, and an ability to think clearly and then act appropriately, is a far more effective response to threatening or dangerous situations.

Should we be in denial?

Others respond by denying the scale of the problems at hand. Instead, they simply maintain a sunny (but unfounded) optimism that everything will inevitably turn out ok in the end.

The problem with this response is that it can fail to take life's problems seriously. We know that it is not a good idea to ignore physical symptoms that could be a mark of an as yet undiagnosed condition. Failure to take such things seriously could have disastrous consequences for our physical health down the line. In the same way, there are many genuine concerns that we might have about other areas of our life, about society or about the world as a whole.

As I reflect on these things as a Christian, I have found that my faith does not make me *less* but *more* concerned about these issues. A developed Christian faith will lead a person to express concerns about many issues that cross traditional party-political boundaries. Instead of seeing the potential issues on only one side of a political debate, such a Christian becomes increasingly concerned about issues on both sides.[152]

Christian hope

I would suggest that the Christian faith is marked by neither pessimistic despair nor unfounded optimism, but by *hope*. In fact, this hope should be the very thing that marks out a Christian.

Peter was one of the first followers of Jesus and a leader of the first-century church. Writing to some Christians who were suffering from massive upheaval and uncertainty, he urges them, 'Always be prepared to give an answer to everyone who asks you to give the reason for the hope that you have.'[153] In other words, he says that Christians should be identified by hope. Many of the Christians Peter is addressing were effectively living as refugees, with no certainty of the immediate future. Nevertheless, Peter suggests that those around them will be able to notice the hope that they exhibit.

I have found that genuine hope, especially in the middle of difficult circumstances, can be incredibly intriguing to those watching on. Once, I was invited to have dinner with a friend's nephew. My friend was a Christian, but his nephew was not. He was, however, very interested to talk about Christianity, and we spent a fascinating evening chatting through his questions. At the end, I asked him how he had come to be so interested. He explained that a work colleague had recently died of cancer. She was the same age as him and had left behind a young family. He continued, 'She was a Christian, and I could see that through everything she had this incredible sense of hope. I want to know what it is that can give someone hope, even in a situation like that.'

Peter explains what the Christian hope is in a second letter. It is not simply an expectation for some disembodied continuation of life after death in another place. Rather, he says, 'But in keeping with his promise we are looking forward to a new heaven and a new earth.'[154]

The sense of the word he uses here for 'new' is not that it *replaces* the old (like getting a new phone), but rather that it *renews* and transforms the old (like a new kitchen or a new garden). The biblical hope, expressed not only here but throughout the Bible, is that one day, God will restore and transform this broken and hurting world and make all things new.

C.S. Lewis captured this concept beautifully in *The Last Battle*, his final book of the Narnia series. In it, the children think they are witnessing the final destruction of the Narnian world that they have grown to know and love. But just at the moment when they feel that all hope is lost, they find themselves in a new world. After a few moments of confusion, they suddenly realise where they are: in the same Narnia that they have just left, but one that is renewed. It has been made even more beautiful and real than the one they had known before. As one of the characters exclaims, 'Kings and Queens ... we have all been blind. We are only beginning to see where we are. From up there I have seen it all ... Narnia is not dead. This is Narnia.'[155]

Christian hope is not about escaping from this world, but about the transformation of this world. It is not about the denial of darkness and death, but about the defeat of darkness and the destruction of death.

Such an incredible vision of the future naturally raises several questions.

The Christian hope is transformative

Talking about a future hope of a transformed world could be seen by some as another form of denial or escapism. How does such a hope really help us in the day-to-day challenges of life? In fact, could it not lead to passivity in the face of the real challenges that we face in the here and now? Actually, I want to suggest that the Christian hope gives us not only great emotional benefits, but also the strongest possible motivation to be actively involved in working for good today.

All of us know how our hopes and expectations for the future affect our emotional state in the present. On the most basic level, we know that if we are going on holiday somewhere sunny next week, we will feel cheerful today, even if it is raining (which is probable if we live in the UK). Positive expectations about the future can lift our emotions in the present – whether it is the prospect of a new job, the approach of one's wedding day, a long-planned-for retirement or news of the manufacture of a vaccine to fight a global pandemic. Even though our present physical circumstances may not yet have changed, the hope that such things offer does change our emotional state.

If these things can bring us joy, how much more would the knowledge that one day everything will be made new? This is why Peter can write to people who are suffering and say, 'In all this you greatly rejoice, though now for a little while you may have to suffer grief in all kinds of trials.'[156] Hope in the future brings joy in the present.

Yet hope doesn't just give us joy; it should also be the greatest motivator to action. Indeed, many of those who have made the greatest difference in our world have been those who have been inspired by hope.

A great example of hope leading to action is found in one of the most famous speeches of all time. Standing on the steps of the Lincoln Memorial in Washington DC, Martin Luther King didn't proclaim, 'I have a nightmare' and describe an apocalyptic vision of future discord in an attempt to scare people into action. Rather, he told the world, 'I have a dream.' It was a dream that was shaped by the Bible's vision of the future, where there won't just be complete equality, but also real unity. Martin Luther King's vision for where history was ultimately heading caused him to strive to make a difference in the world in his day.

The Christian vision of the future has led many to take action and change the world for good. Christians, inspired by the hope that one day all sickness will be healed and death defeated, have opened hospitals and pioneered health care across the world. Christians, who believe that one day the knowledge of God will fill the earth, have established schools and universities to increase people's knowledge today. It was Christians, who believed in a day of final freedom for all people, who led the fight to abolish the slave trade. There are many Christians today who believe that creation will one day be set free from decline and, as a result, are working to care for that creation through their environmental concern.

No other belief system gives you such hope for our world. Other religions may hold out hope for some spiritual paradise, but that doesn't involve this world, and therefore doesn't give the same motivation to make a difference in it today. The secular, atheistic viewpoint lacks this level of motivation as, ultimately, it believes we must face up to the reality that not only we but everything will be destroyed. Atheism considers our actions today to be like attempts to keep patching up an old car that is ultimately destined for the scrap heap. We might be able to prolong its life a little with some care and attention, but that is all. However, if Christianity is true, then making a positive difference in the world is not only what we want to do and what feels intuitively right, but actually *is* what we should do. We don't have to try to change the world while ignoring the ultimate nature of reality and pretending things are otherwise. Instead, we can discover that the true nature of reality makes sense of both our deepest desires and how our world is.

The Christian hope is real

A second objection to this description of Christian hope could be that it sounds too good to be true. We are used to being sceptical about online deals offering us thousands of pounds from an overseas bank account. We wisely learn that if something sounds too good to be true, then it probably is. Yet while a healthy degree of scepticism can protect us, too much scepticism could cause us to miss out on something real.

A couple of days ago, my wife showed me an email offering her a £50 Amazon voucher from a person whose name she didn't recognise. I immediately suggested she disregard it as spam. Thankfully, she is more thorough than I am and, after a little investigation, discovered that it was, in fact, authentic – a genuine thank-you gift for something she had done, from someone she had never actually met! My default scepticism nearly caused her to miss out on what was rightfully hers.

In the same way, it is easy to dismiss the amazing biblical vision of the future without looking into it. How can Peter talk about such an incredible, joy-giving, life-changing, world-altering hope? At the start of his first letter, he explains how: 'Praise be to the God and Father of our Lord Jesus Christ! In his great mercy he has given us new birth into a living hope through the resurrection of Jesus Christ from the dead.'[157] Jesus' resurrection is the basis for Christian hope. Our hope in the future is rooted in an event in the past.

Perhaps we think we should be sceptical about such an unusual claim. When I was talking with a student on this subject, he exclaimed, 'Resurrection! Things like that don't happen every day!'

I smiled.

'Exactly!' I responded. 'If they did, then we wouldn't be talking about Jesus today, would we?'

The Christian belief in the resurrection of Jesus is a claim about a unique event in history, but that doesn't mean it couldn't have happened. The event popularly known as 'The Big Bang' is also claimed to be a unique and unrepeated event, but is believed to have happened because we can extrapolate back to it from the evidence we see in the universe today. In the same way, we need to examine the initial 'explosion' of Jesus' resurrection from the dead that is still reverberating around the world today. How do you get from Jesus being crucified on a cross at the hands of his enemies to the global domination of the Christian church today?

Another source of our scepticism might be the unlikeliness of a dead person coming to life. After all, *we* know that dead people stay dead, but so too did people just over 2000 years ago. You don't need a degree in medicine to establish that!

Similarly, if we think that the idea of a deceased person rising from the dead is too hard to believe, it is worth realising that many people already believe something even more incredible. If there is no God behind the universe, we have to believe that all life that exists originally came from non-life. Not only that, but we also have to believe that everything that exists ultimately came from nothing at all. It turns out we all believe in miracles; the question is just *which* miracle?

A good reason for believing in Jesus' resurrection is that, as unlikely as it initially sounds, the evidence of history points in the direction of it being true. Indeed, as one scholar put it, we have 'a great hole in history, a hole the shape and size of the resurrection'.[158]

A good friend of mine was a student in Bristol and part of the Christian student group there. One Easter, they decided to organise what they called 'The Great Resurrection Debate'. They took out a double-page spread in the student newspaper that asked people to submit a written theory of how they might explain away the evidence for the resurrection of Jesus in naturalistic terms. The best suggestions, it explained, would then be shortlisted, and the entrants invited to present their case at a cheese and wine evening in the Student Union. A local high court judge was invited to adjudicate the event.

The newspaper ad also outlined some of the evidence. In particular, it focused on five established facts that almost all scholars – Christian, Jewish or atheist – could agree upon:

1. Jesus Christ was crucified. This event is also recorded outside of the New Testament documents and is one of the most well-established facts of ancient history.

2. Jesus' tomb was found to be empty. If it hadn't been, then Christianity could never have begun. There is no record of anyone doubting the fact of the empty tomb for at least 200 years after the event. What is more, even the enemies of the Christian faith allude to the empty tomb when they decide to circulate a story of the disciples stealing the body.[159]

3. The followers of Jesus were convinced that they had met Jesus alive again after his crucifixion. This was not something they could have likely made up, as all of them suffered, and many of them died, for the belief. While people may die for things that aren't true, they generally don't die for things that they *know* aren't true. Jesus' followers were utterly convinced by something.

4. The lives of Jesus' followers were transformed by the belief that Jesus rose from the dead. Even those who had previously been sceptical or even hostile (like James and Paul) became convinced followers after this event.

5. The Christian church exploded right across the Roman Empire over the next decades, in spite of opposition and, at times, severe persecution. This movement was based on the claim that Jesus was alive, and the movement spread at a time when the eye-witnesses were still alive.

Many individuals entered the Christian students' competition, spurred on by the incentive of the £500 cash prize (a decent amount for a cash-strapped student!). The shortlisted candidates came to present their case. At the event, two interesting things happened.

The winner had come up with a theory that Jesus hadn't really died on the cross, but had simply passed out and then revived in the tomb. However, as he went up to claim his prize, he admitted that he wasn't even convinced himself by his own argument (though he was very thankful for the cash!). A few weeks later, he became a Christian after becoming convinced that the only reasonable explanation was that Jesus actually did rise from the dead.

Secondly, the high court judge, in his closing remarks, commented that none of the explanations given would have stood up in a court of law. All of them would have been thrown out for none of them satisfactorily explained all the evidence.

Many others have attempted to explain away the evidence for the resurrection and have met similar barriers, which is why no one explanation has really stuck, despite 200 years of critical examination and scholarship. Indeed, some of those who have attempted to account for the resurrection, like that student, have had to change their mind once confronted by the evidence. What seems absurd at first to our secular Western minds actually becomes convincing the more we look into it.

Jesus' resurrection is not based on some psychological wish fulfilment. It is based on solid evidence.

The Christian hope needs to be personally embraced

A third objection to the Christian hope is that if Jesus offers such hope for our world, why doesn't he bring about this reality now? Why do we have to go on living in this broken and struggling world full of injustice and pain? Does he not care?

The answer is quite the opposite. Anticipating those very questions, Peter explains why this ultimate hope has not yet been realised: 'The Lord is not slow in keeping his promise, as some understand slowness. Instead he is patient with you, not wanting anyone to perish, but everyone to come to repentance.'[160] God's delay in transforming this world is not because he doesn't care, but because he *does* – with patience.

One day, God will transform this broken world. He will get rid of all that is now rubbish and all that spoils it. He will bring perfect justice. But that begs an honest question and needs an honest answer. What about the rubbish in my life? What about the stuff I do that spoils the world for others? If I want God to bring justice, what does that mean for me?

The reality is that if God were to get rid of everything that spoils this world, he would have to also get rid of *us*. In so many ways, we can be part of the problem. We may not physically fight wars with guns, but our words can cause real pain and create conflict with those around us. We may not traffic women into sex slavery, but we can still choose to access websites that create demand for such a destructive industry. We may not be guilty of perpetrating a genocide, but we can choose to turn a blind eye to horrors that are happening right now and continue to give implicit support to the countries where such crimes are perpetrated. We may be quick to publicly show our support for whatever cause has gained traction on social media, but much slower to put our money where our mouth is, or to do anything more than repost what others have already said.

The truth is that before God changes the world, he needs to change us. Wonderfully, because of Jesus, we can experience that transformation. Through Jesus' death on the cross, we can experience God's forgiveness. Because of Jesus' powerful resurrection, we can know his power at work in us, changing us from within.

To experience this, we need to turn back to God, acknowledging where we have gone wrong and reorientating our lives towards God. This is what Peter means when he talks about 'to come to repentance'. It is a whole new way of thinking. How might we do that?

Are we willing to do so? It is to these final questions we must now turn.

Conclusion

Picture the scene. Rob has just started at university. During his first few weeks of lectures, he has been somewhat distracted from his studies in quantum mechanics by Kirstie. She is on the same course and normally sits a couple of rows in front of him. Eventually, he plucks up the courage to get chatting to her and a friendship develops. They start to hang out outside of lectures and, in Rob's mind, things seem to be progressing well. Putting aside his early attempts at budgeting, he books a table for two at one of the most exclusive restaurants in town. After a delicious three-course meal, they find themselves walking by the seafront. The reflected moonlight is dancing on the water and a warm, autumnal breeze is blowing. They pause to sit and look out on the view.

After a few moments, the silence is broken by Rob's voice, which sounds more hesitant than normal. 'Kirstie,' he begins, turning to look at her. 'There's something I've been wanting to say for a while.' She turns to look at him and sees that he's looking rather nervous. 'Well,' he continues, 'here's the thing. I think … well … I just want to say … I love you.'

There's a moment's pause as Kirstie takes in what Rob has just said. How will she respond? What will she say? We might expect her to respond in one of three ways.

She could look rather shocked and explain to Rob he's misunderstood her intentions in spending time together. She just saw this as a platonic friendship. She enjoys spending time with him, but doesn't see it as developing into anything more.

Alternatively, she might be rather surprised and ask for some time to think. She doesn't yet know how she feels about him and wants to get to know him more before she could see where it might lead.

Finally, there is a third response – the one that Rob is hoping for. She may respond fast by saying, 'I love you too!'

Of course, we don't know how she will respond, as Kirstie and Rob don't really exist; I just made them up. But in such a scenario, we do know what Kirstie *would not* say. After Rob declaring his love for Kirstie, it would be very strange if she were to simply respond with, 'That's nice' before walking off – as if he were merely commenting on the weather or similar. Faced with Rob's declaration of love, she could reject it (for that is the risk that he takes by declaring his love); she could take time to reflect on it (for relationships *can* take time); or she could receive it with a positive response to it.

My purpose in telling such a story is not to offer relationship advice. (Despite recently getting married, I don't count myself an expert in that area – just very blessed!) However, the story illustrates the kinds of ways we might also respond to Jesus' offer to satisfy our longings, to meet our deepest needs, to give us a secure basis to our identity and to provide a strong foundation to our lives.

In writing this book, I have sought to show how Jesus makes best sense of what matters most in life. We have seen how, in spite of everything, God loves us and wants us to be closely connected to him. We have seen what that cost God to achieve – only through the death and resurrection of Jesus can we find the love and companionship that we desperately need. In Jesus, our guilt can melt away like the snow in the springtime. In Jesus, we can find true security and a strong foundation to life, which enables us to choose joy even when life is hard. He wants to partner with us to bring about good and to work for justice in this hurting world. So how will we respond?

As in my story of the love proposal above, there are several different ways that we *could* respond. But the one thing we really shouldn't say is, 'That's nice' – as if Jesus were simply another optional course in self-improvement. The claims of Christianity that we have examined through this book are too extensive and impact us too individually for us to simply dismiss them as 'nice'. That leaves us with three possible responses.

Reject?

One way that individuals can respond to the Christian faith is to reject it. We might do this *explicitly*, like the atheist who is willing to hang part of their identity on their open rejection of Christianity. On the other hand, we might do it more *implicitly* by simply choosing to ignore it or think no more about it.

Before I too quickly challenge such a response, I want to point out that the fact we can even choose to reject Christianity tells us something significant about it. The Christian faith is at heart an invitation into a relationship with the God who made us and knows us. Like any relationship of real love, there has to be the choice of whether to accept or reject it to make it real. Christians would say that God has created us as responsible beings and that part of our essential dignity is our freedom to choose responsibly. It would be a total contradiction of what Christianity actually is all about to try to force someone to be a Christian. That is why, I think, it is no accident that there is a high correlation between the level of political and religious freedom in different parts of the world and the influence of Christianity upon them.

However, just because we *can* reject the Christian faith doesn't mean that we should! I can fully understand why you may want to reject some expressions of traditional religion, such as the church or even some individual professing Christians that you have met. However, let me ask what it is about Jesus himself that you might want to reject? As I said at the start of this book, *Christ*ianity is primarily about Christ. Even if the church has let Christ down throughout history, I hope, at the very least, you would be willing to consider him further. Why not start with one of the contemporary biographies of his life (the four gospels: Matthew, Mark, Luke and John) and read it through? There are good reasons for not taking the gospel accounts as some sort of religious make-believe, but as real, well-documented history. In addition, while some history may seem dusty, dull and irrelevant, Jesus is the most captivating figure in history and of supreme relevance to each one of us.

If you're still tempted to think no more of Christianity, then to where else are you going to turn to make sense of life? We have seen that Jesus makes best sense of the things that matter most. How are you otherwise going to account for both the beauty and the brokenness of our world? Where else are you going to ground your concern for human rights, the environment and other issues of social justice? And where are you going to find a secure basis for love, happiness, freedom and hope?

Reflect?

Perhaps, though, you are genuinely intrigued by what you have discovered about Jesus so far, but still have significant questions. You would therefore like to explore his story more before you decide what you think.

Given the magnitude of Jesus' claims, and the huge repercussions for every area of our lives if they are true, then it would be very sensible to think deeply and carefully about them. There is much more to say about each area covered in this book, so do check out my recommended reading for suggestions of where to go to look into any of the topics in more detail. As already mentioned, the best way to consider the claims of Christianity more carefully is to read through one of the accounts of Jesus' life, if you haven't already done so.

Why not also find a regular opportunity to examine these things more closely? If someone recommended this book to you, then maybe chat to them for ideas. Many churches provide a forum for asking questions about Christianity and offer help with reading about Jesus in the Bible. Alternatively, do feel free to get in touch with me directly at michaelots.com – I would be glad to put you in touch with a helpful church in your area or to respond to any questions you might have.

Receive?

While it is good to reflect more deeply on the issues raised in this book, it would be a mistake to use that as an excuse to indefinitely put off making up your mind! G.K. Chesterton, the writer and theologian, observed, 'Merely having an open mind is nothing. The object of opening the mind, as of opening the mouth, is to shut it again on something solid.'[161]

Don't assume that you need to have had every question answered and have delved into every topic in detail before you can get started with the Christian faith. You don't! Indeed, the joy of being a Christian is a relationship with and knowledge of God *himself*. This lifetime alone is not long enough to fully discover everything there is to know about him and about his world that he has made for us to enjoy! Amazingly, the Christian has an eternity for this process and so expects their life to be one of perpetual discovery. The question, therefore, is not whether you understand *everything* (you never will), but rather do you understand enough about Jesus to want to entrust your life to him and get to know him more fully?

As being a Christian is all about having a relationship with God, we can't fully know what that will mean for our lives. The Christian life is not like taking up a new hobby, buying a new pet or discovering a new area of study. It is more like getting married – it changes everything (or, at least, it should!). Nor will it always be easy. In fact, for the majority of Christians in non-Western countries, it may be incredibly costly. But while there is a cost, ultimately there is more to lose from *not* following Jesus than there is from following him – that is, by becoming a Christian. There is far more to gain from living life *with* him than there is from anything that we might need to give up.

So how do you begin as a Christian? Throughout this book, I have been talking about God and what he has done for us. Why not end your reading session by talking to God directly? You could start with some of the simplest words that we ever learn: sorry, thank you and please.

You could say *sorry* for the way you have kept God out of your life so far, and for the way you have hurt him and others through what you have sometimes done or neglected to do.

You could say *thank you* that despite how you have often rejected him, God has not rejected you. Thank him for his love for you, shown in Jesus' death on the cross, and for the offer of a fresh start that he gives to all.

Then say to God, *please* will you come into my life, through your Holy Spirit, and feature in all of it, every day. Ask him to give you the freedom, joy, love and companionship that he offers.

Living life with Jesus

Saying and meaning such a prayer is not so much the end of your investigation into Christianity, but the beginning of a new life *with Jesus*! On one occasion, Jesus said, 'I have come that they may have life, and have it to the full.'[162] The joy of being a Christian is that we have come to know the one who is the *source* of life and who makes *sense* of life. This doesn't just change the way we think; it should then visibly change the way we live.

Knowing the God who created us with dignity and value should lead us to treat others in the same way, and work for equality and justice for all.

Knowing the Creator of everything motivates us to care for his world.

Knowing that there is more to life than personal happiness should free us to live for things that are meaningful – and, ironically, help us discover happiness as a result.

Knowing the root cause of our world's divisions should help us to build bridges and bring healing and reconciliation.

Knowing the God who suffered with us, and for us, means that we can work in deep partnership with him to bring about good in this hurting world.

Knowing that our identity finds its ultimate foundation in God gives our lives a stable foundation that allows us to discover intimately just *who* we were created to be.

Knowing that we are never truly alone allows us to enjoy times of solitude, but also to reach out to others in self-giving friendship.

Knowing the ultimate freedom that Jesus brings in releasing us from our prisons should empower us to work to bring freedom to others.

Knowing the source of love means we not only get to enjoy his love, but also to show it to others.

Confident in Jesus' resurrection and knowing he is alive, we can face what sometimes seems an uncertain future with security, confidence and hope.

Jesus really does makes best sense of the things that matter most!

Further reading

Bennet, David, *A War of Loves: The Unexpected Story of a Gay Activist Discovering Jesus* (Zondervan, 2018)

Dirckx, Sharon, *Am I Just My Brain?* (The Good Book Company, 2019)

Harrison, Glynn, *A Better Story: God, Sex and Human Flourishing* (IVP, 2017)

Harrison, Glynn, *The Big Ego Trip: Finding True Significance in a Culture of Self-Esteem* (IVP, 2013)

Holland, Tom, *Dominion: The Making of the Western Mind* (Abacus, 2020)

Keller, Tim, *Making Sense of God: An Invitation to the Sceptical* (Hodder and Stoughton, 2018)

Lennox, John, *Can Science Explain Everything?* (The Good Book Company, 2019)

Lukianoff, Greg and Jonathan Haidt, *The Coddling of the American Mind: How Good Intentions and Bad Ideas Are Setting Up a Generation for Failure* (Penguin, 2019)

McLaughlin, Rebecca, *The Secular Creed: Engaging Five Contemporary Claims* (TGC, 2021)

Orr-Ewing, Amy, *Where Is God in All the Suffering?* (The Good Book Company, 2020)

Ots, Michael, *But Is It True?: Honest Responses to 10 Popular Objections to the Christian Faith* (IVP, 2016)

Ots, Michael, *What Kind of God?: Responses to 10 Popular Accusations* (IVP, 2008)

Ots, Michael, *What Kind of Hope?: How Jesus Changes Everything* (IVP, 2012)

Sprinkle, Preston, *Embodied: Transgender Identities, the Church, and What the Bible Has to Say* (David C. Cook, 2021)

Notes

Introduction

1   Paul Kalanithi, *When Breath Becomes Air* (Vintage, 2017), p. 168.

2   Paul Kalanithi, *When Breath Becomes Air*, p. 169.

3   Michael Ots, *But Is It True?* (IVP, 2016).

1. Making sense of humanity

4   Francis Crick, *The Astonishing Hypothesis* (Touchstone, 1995), p. 3.

5   *The New Republic*, 28 May 2008; https://newrepublic.com/article/64674/the-stupidity-dignity

6   Yuval Noah Harari, *Sapiens* (Vintage, 2015), p. 124.

7   Quoted in *The Guardian*, 6 November 1999; https://www.theguardian.com/lifeandstyle/1999/nov/06/weekend.kevintoolis

8   Tom Holland, *Dominion: The Making of the Western Mind* (Little, Brown Book Group, 2019).

9   https://www.youtube.com/watch?v=7eSyz3BaVK8

10   Mark 2:1–12.

11   Yuval Noah Harari, *Sapiens*, p. 122. It is worth noting that while Harari talks about people having a divinely created soul, it would be more accurate to say that we *are* divinely created souls. The division of the physical and spiritual owes more to Ancient Greek thought than the Bible.

12   Genesis 1:27.

13   https://www.archives.gov/founding-docs/declaration-transcript. Many of the Founding Fathers were deists and would not have held to most other Christians beliefs. However, they built an entire civilisation on this one.

14   See Mark 2:13–17.

15   See Mark 1:40–45.

16   C.S. Lewis, *The Last Battle* (HarperCollins, 1998), p. 205.

17   J John, Twitter, https://twitter.com/canonjjohn/status/315443369381863425.

18   This particular talk was not recorded, but the illustration is used with the speaker's permission.

19   Mark 2:9.

2. Making sense of our world

20 https://blog.arocha.org/en/extinction-the-facts-a-rocha-responds-in-hope-action/

21 As quoted by Richard Dawkins, *The God Delusion* (Bantam, 2006), p. 288.

22 See Genesis 2:15.

23 See surah 7:24–25 in the Quran.

24 Jim Irwin, *More than Earthlings: An Astronaut's Thoughts for Christ-Centered Living* (Baptist Sunday School Board, 1983).

25 Some might argue that the Bible teaches that this world will be destroyed, quoting 2 Peter 3:11 as saying that everything 'will be destroyed'. However, this would contradict the clear teaching of other parts of the Bible like Romans 8:21 that speak of creation being liberated from decay. When the Bible speaks of a new earth, it is using the word in the sense of 'renew' rather than 'replace'. In light of this, it makes much more sense to read the words of 2 Peter as saying that it is evil that will be destroyed and not the physical world itself. For more on this, see my book *What Kind of Hope?* (IVP, 2012).

26 Do check out Kieran's stunning photographs and a longer explanation of this story at https://www.kierandodds.com/work/hierotopia/

27   https://www.arocha.org/en/

28   See Yuval Noah Harari, *Sapiens* (Vintage, 2011),
      pp. 104–105. Harari admits, 'From a narrow
      evolutionary perspective … the agricultural
      revolution was a wonderful boon for chickens,
      cattle, pigs and sheep.' Yet he fails to explain how,
      if we are the result of the evolutionary process,
      we can appeal to anything outside of it for our
      understanding of what is right and wrong.

29   Interestingly, BT had to apologise after it became
      clear that this slogan had already been used by
      another company; https://www.thetimes.co.uk/
      article/start-up-tech-will-save-us-accuses-bt-of-
      pinching-its-slogan-hpmkwct3r

30   As quoted on the *Huffington Post*, 22 August 2014;
      https://web.archive.org/web/20160105052014/
      http://www.huffingtonpost.co.uk/daniel-crockett/
      nature-connection-will-be-the-next-big-human-
      trend_b_5698267.html

31   https://www.theguardian.com/
      environment/2019/apr/23/greta-thunberg-full-
      speech-to-mps-you-did-not-act-in-time

32   I also find such pessimistic predictions slightly ironic
      given that it was Christians who used to be accused
      of scaremongering – when they predicted that 'the
      end of the world is nigh'. One of the objections of

the New Atheists to Christianity was the negative emotional impact they perceived that such fear about the future would have on children.

33 https://www.totallyveganbuzz.com/news/lewis-hamilton-says-the-world-is-messed-up-because-of-meat-industry/

34 Quoted from an extract published in *The Times* magazine, 13 March 2021.

35 John 20:11–18.

36 See Revelation 21–22.

37 https://www.newstatesman.com/politics/energy/2017/10/christiana-figueres-why-i-chose-optimism-over-climate-doom

38 https://www.arocha.or.ke/projects/assets/ and https://www.assets-kenya.org/

3. Making sense of happiness

39 From 'Brits Love to be Miserable: US Bestseller', a review in *The Observer*, 9 March 2008.

40 Ibid.

41 https://worldhappiness.report/

42 Oliver James, *Affluenza* (Vermillion, 2007).

43   Jonathan Haidt, *The Happiness Hypothesis* (Basic Books, 2006).

44   Tal Ben-Shahar, *Happier: Learn the Secrets to Daily Joy and Lasting Fulfilment* (McGraw-Hill Education, 2007).

45   https://www.telegraph.co.uk/books/ what-to-read/40-quotes-about-life-for-a- pessimist/jim-carrey-/

46   Tal Ben-Shaha, *The Question of Happiness: On Finding Meaning, Pleasure, and the Ultimate Currency* (iUniverse, 2002), p. 15.

47   For anyone wishing to undertake a similar cycle expedition, I have one piece of advice. Before you apply cooling balm to relieve the symptoms of saddle soreness, check that you haven't actually been mis-sold a cream that has quite the opposite effect!

48   Yuval Noah Harari, *Sapiens* (Vintage, 2011), p. 436.

49   I realise that Jordan Peterson is a marmite-like figure – some people love him; others hate him. Yet all of us need to ask how has someone who gives incredibly long YouTube lectures, with little interaction and no visual aids, been found so compelling by so many people?

50   Jordan B. Peterson, *12 Rules for Life: An Antidote to Chaos* (Allen Lane, 2018), p. 161.

51 The subtitle of Jonathan Haidt's book is: *Putting Ancient Wisdom and Philosophy to the Test of Modern Science*.

52 Mark 10:17–22.

53 https://www.youtube.com/watch?v=C8h4s_bGkro

54 Tal Ben-Shaha, *The Question of Happiness*, p. 15.

55 John 17:3.

56 John 10:10.

57 C.S. Lewis, *The Weight of Glory* (HarperCollins, 2001), p. 26.

58 Mark 10:18. I have spoken with Muslim friends who believe that by saying this, Jesus was denying any claim that he was God. This, though, would cut against the rest of his teaching, where he makes repeated claims to deity. In this particular situation, it seems that Jesus is encouraging the man to consider that rather than being just good, he could be more than good. In the same way, I would want to encourage my Muslim friends to consider whether Jesus might also be more than a good teacher and a revered prophet. As God, he shows us what true goodness looks like. I may also want to ask my Muslim friends, 'If you don't believe that Jesus was God, are you happy to concede that he, by his own reckoning, wasn't good?'

59 Mark 8:35–36.

60 There is a real irony that while Jesus didn't pursue greatness, but rather chose a path of humble service, no one has ever achieved more greatness than Jesus!

61 2 Corinthians 8:9.

62 C.S. Lewis, *Surprised by Joy* (Fount, 1977), p. 182.

63 C.S. Lewis, *Mere Christianity* (Fontana, 1956), p. 116.

4. Making sense of society

64 A shocking example of this is what happened at Evergreen State College in Washington, US. See Greg Lukianoff and Jonathan Haidt, *The Coddling of the American Mind* (Allen Lane, 2018), pp. 114–19.

65 Douglas Murray, *The Madness of Crowds* (Bloomsbury, 2019).

66 Greg Lukianoff and Jonathan Haidt, *The Coddling of the American Mind*.

67 https://www.politics.co.uk/week-in-review/2021/03/19/week-in-review-right-and-left-have-succumbed-to-the-outrage-machine/?cmpredirect

68 It is easy for some to dismiss such things as evidence of the existence of a *snowflake generation* – a people who are so fragile that they cannot cope with ideas they disagree with. Yet when you witness some of

the hostility with which the debates are conducted, you can understand why some may want to have a *safe space* away from them or at very least be given *trigger warnings* to prepare them for potentially divisive or painful content.

69   https://harpers.org/a-letter-on-justice-and-open-debate/

70   Kate Fox, *Watching the English* (John Murray, 2004).

71   Greg Lukianoff and Jonathan Haidt, *The Coddling of the American Mind*, p. 19.

72   Greg Lukianoff and Jonathan Haidt, *The Coddling of the American Mind*, p. 20.

73   Greg Lukianoff and Jonathan Haidt, *The Coddling of the American Mind*, p. 33.

74   Greg Lukianoff and Jonathan Haidt, *The Coddling of the American Mind*, p. 53.

75   https://www.theguardian.com/commentisfree/2019/nov/01/does-obamas-critique-of-radical-politics-help-bring-about-the-change-he-wanted

76   Alexander Solzhenitsyn, *The Gulag Archipelago* (Harvill, 2003), p. 75.

77   Greg Lukianoff and Jonathan Haidt, *The Coddling of the American Mind*, p. 264.

78   Stephen Pinker, *Enlightenment Now* (Penguin, 2018).

79   It is worth reading the quote in its wider context: '"Not all of the Enlightenment thinkers were atheists", he says early on. He's right, in a sense. Spinoza wasn't. Locke wasn't. Newton wasn't. Hobbes wasn't (but really who knows with Hobbes). Boyle wasn't. Voltaire wasn't. Hume wasn't. Gibbon wasn't. Kant wasn't. Paine wasn't. Priestley wasn't. La Mettrie, Baron d'Holbach and Bentham definitely were. Diderot, Helvetius and d'Alembert hovered. Others, like Cesare Beccaria, a now much-neglected Enlightenment thinker, whom Pinker rightly admires for his proposals to reform penal law along rational and proportional lines, was scared away from d'Holbach's salon by its atheism. Under no stretching of the imagination could the Enlightenment be imagined to be an atheistic movement, for which Pinker is clearly straining to claim it.' Indeed, it is well worth reading the whole review! https://www.theosthinktank.co.uk/comment/2018/02/20/enlightenment-and-progress-or-why-steven-pinker-is-wrong

80   Tom Holland, *Dominion: The Making of the Western Mind* (Little, Brown Book Group, 2019).

81   To read the whole account, go to Mark 7:1–23.

82   Jon Ronson, *So You've Been Publicly Shamed* (Riverhead Books, 2015), p. 86.

83   Jon Ronson, *So You've Been Publicly Shamed*, p. 275.

84   Martin Lewis, on his MartinSLewis Twitter account, 9 October 2018; https://twitter.com/MartinSLewis/status/1049589289854689285

85   https://www.politics.co.uk/week-in-review/2021/03/19/week-in-review-right-and-left-have-succumbed-to-the-outrage-machine/?cmpredirect

86   Douglas Murray, *The Madness of Crowds*, p. 182.

5. Making sense of suffering

87   David Benatar, *The Human Predicament* (Oxford University Press, 2017), p. 63.

88   As quoted by Amanda Lohrey, 'The Big Nothing: Lawrence Krauss and Arse-Kicking Physics', *The Monthly*, October 2012; https://www.themonthly.com.au/issue/2012/october/1354074365/amanda-lohrey/big-nothing#mtr

89   Alex Rosenburg, *The Atheist's Guide to Reality* (W.W. Norton and Company, 2012), p. 2.

90   Romans 8:28.

91   Romans 8:18.

92   Romans 8:20.

93   Romans 8:22.

94   Romans 8:20–21 and 23.

95   https://www.bbc.co.uk/news/uk-wales-55362437

96   Romans 8:28, NKJV.

97   Psalm 73.

98   Romans 8:28, NIV.

99   Because of the ordering of words in Greek, there
     is occasionally some ambiguity about how best
     to translate a verse. Both previous translations
     of this verse are legitimate possibilities. Where
     there is uncertainty, a good guide is to see which
     rendering fits best with the rest of what the Bible
     says. For a detailed discussion about why the
     following is the best translation of this particular
     verse, see http://thinktheology.org/2014/04/02/
     revisiting-romans-828/

100 This alternative translation is suggested in the NIV's
     footnote to Romans 8:28.

101 https://www.thegospelcoalition.org/blogs/justin-
     taylor/jesus-of-scars/

102 A translation suggested in the NIV's footnote
     to Romans 8:28.

6. Making sense of myself

103 On one occasion, she was on her way to the flight
     deck when one of the business-class passengers
     asked her for a glass of champagne. She replied,

'I'm afraid they don't let me near the alcohol for obvious reasons, but I will ask one of the cabin crew to bring one to you.'

104 Luke 19:1–10.

105 Interestingly, we are told the exact type of tree that he climbed – a sycamore-fig tree. Such incidental detail is typical of authentic eye-witness testimony. In fact, as the Bible scholar Peter Williams points out, this type of tree is very specific to that geographical area, lending further weight to the fact that this testimony came from someone who was there. This is just one of hundreds of small details which, cumulatively, form a compelling case for taking the gospel accounts as reliable sources. For more on this, check out: Peter Williams, *Can We Trust the Gospels?* (Crossway, 2018).

106 For a number of years, I had the privilege of working with a community in Eastern Europe. We spent much of our time going into people's homes for simple meals, or even just a drink. I was astonished to learn that many of the families had been excitedly anticipating our visit for days. Our going to their home was seen as showing dignity and respect to people who have often been despised and rejected.

107 David Foster Wallace, *This Is Water: Some Thoughts, Delivered on a Significant Occasion, about*

Living a Compassionate Life (Little, Brown Book Group, 2009), p. 98.

108 *Cool Runnings* (Walt Disney, 1993).

109 Luke 19:9–10.

110 For a really helpful, clear and empathetic discussion of this subject, I highly recommend reading Preston Sprinkle, *Embodied: Transgender Identities, the Church, and What the Bible Has to Say* (David C. Cook, 2021).

7. Making sense of loneliness

111 'Britain the loneliness capital of Europe', *The Telegraph*, 18 June 2014; https://www.telegraph.co.uk/lifestyle/wellbeing/10909524/Britain-the-loneliness-capital-of-Europe.html

112 This is according to findings presented to the Annual Convention of the American Psychological Association; https://www.triplem.com.au/story/lonely-people-50-more-likely-to-die-early-49122

113 Fay Bound Alberti, *A Biography of Loneliness* (OUP Oxford, 2019), p. 10.

114 https://www.rebeccamclaughlin.org/post/2018/07/21/is-church-literally-good-for-you

115 John 1:1–5, 9–14.

116 Glen Scrivener, *321: The Story of God, the World and You* (10Publishing, 2014), p. 55.

117　John 1:14.

118　See John 8:58 where Jesus refers to himself as the 'I am', echoing the name that God used of himself in Exodus 3:14. The religious leaders listening to Jesus are under no illusions about what Jesus is doing. They react by picking up stones to stone him (John 8:59).

119　Matthew 1:23.

120　Romans 3:10–11.

121　Genesis 2:18.

122　You can get in touch with me via my website www.michaelots.com – I'd love to put you in touch with a helpful church near you.

8. Making sense of freedom

123　'Viva Ned Flanders', episode 10, series 10 of *The Simpsons* (Fox, 1999).

124　John Gray, *Straw Dogs* (Granta Books, 2003), p. 26.

125　*Frozen* (Disney, 2013).

126　John 8:31–36.

127　Francis Spufford, *Unapologetic* (Faber and Faber, 2013), p. 27.

128　First released on John Mayer's live album *Try* (Columbia, 2005).

129 Russell Brand, *Recovery: Freedom from Our Addictions* (Bluebird, 2017), p. 15.

130 https://www.cityam.com/coronavirus-screen-time-soars-as-adults-spend-half-their-day-on-devices

131 https://www.telegraph.co.uk/news/1526206/I-was-in-Hitlers-SS-admits-Gunter-Grass.html

132 Tom Tarrants, *Consumed by Hate, Redeemed by Love* (Thomas Nelson, 2019).

9. Making sense of love

133 Quoted from an article by Sharon Feinstein, 'Rock on Freddie', in *The Sunday Magazine*, 14 April 1985.

134 Robbie Williams, 'Feel', from the album *Escapology* (EMI, 2002).

135 Patricia S. Churchland, 'Epistemology in the Age of Neuroscience', *Journal of Philosophy*, Volume 84, Number 10 (1987), p. 548. Quoted in Timothy Keller, *The Reason for God* (Hodder and Stoughton, 2009), p. 137.

136 Richard Dawkins, *The God Delusion* (Black Swan, 2016), p. 253.

137 Max Korzh, 'Endorfina' (2013). Like almost all music, it sounds much better in the original language!

138 1 John 4:16.

139 Genesis 2:24.

140 Spice Girls, '2 Become 1' (Virgin Records, 1996).

141 Genesis 1:27.

142 This encounter can be found in John 4:1–26.

143 John 4:9.

144 John 4:10.

145 John 4:11.

146 John 4:13–14.

147 John 4:19, 25–26.

148 John 4:26.

149 Genesis 2:18.

10. Making sense of hope

150 https://www.theguardian.com/
     environment/2019/jan/25/our-house-is-on-fire-
     greta-thunberg16-urges-leaders-to-act-on-climate

151 Quoted in Jessica G. Fritze, 'Hope, Despair
     and Transformation: Climate Change and the
     Promotion of Mental Health and Wellbeing'
     in *International Journal of Mental Health Systems*,
     Volume 2, Article 13 (2008).

152 A really helpful *New York Times* article on this, by Christian writer and thinker Timothy Keller, can be found here: https://www.nytimes.com/2018/09/29/opinion/sunday/christians-politics-belief.html

153 1 Peter 3:15.

154 2 Peter 3:13.

155 C.S. Lewis, *The Last Battle* (HarperCollins, 2009), p. 208.

156 1 Peter 1:6.

157 1 Peter 1:3.

158 C.F.D. Moule, *The Phenomenon of the New Testament* (SCM, 1967), p. 3.

159 Matthew 28:13.

160 2 Peter 3:9.

Conclusion

161 G.K. Chesterton, *The Autobiography of G.K. Chesterton* (Sheed & Ward, 1936), pp. 228–29.

162 John 10:10.